1 and 2 Thessal...

Good News Commentaries

1 and 2 Thessalonians

Earl F. Palmer

A GOOD NEWS COMMENTARY

New Testament Editor
W. Ward Gasque

1817

HARPER & ROW, PUBLISHERS, SAN FRANCISCO

Cambridge, Hagerstown, New York, Philadelphia
London, Mexico City, São Paulo, Sydney

To my friends and companions in an exciting vision at New College Berkeley

1 and 2 Thessalonians: A Good News Commentary. Copyright © 1983 by Earl F. Palmer. All rights reserved. Printed in the United States of America. No part of this book may be used or reproduced in any manner whatsoever without written permission except in the case of brief quotations embodied in critical articles and reviews. For information address Harper & Row, Publishers, Inc., 10 East 53rd Street, New York, NY 10022. Published simultaneously in Canada by Fitzhenry & Whiteside, Limited, Toronto.

FIRST EDITION

Designed by Design Office Bruce Kortebein

Library of Congress Cataloging in Publication Data
Palmer, Earl F.
   1 AND 2 THESSALONIANS.

   (A Good News Commentary)
   Bibliography: p.
   Includes indexes.
   1. Bible. N.T. Thessalonians—Commentaries.
I. Title. N.T. Thessalonians. II. Title. III. Series.
BS2725.3.P34   1983   227'.8207'7   82-48409
ISBN 0-06-066455-X

83 84 85 86 87 10 9 8 7 6 5 4 3 2 1

About the Series

This is the first major series to use the popular Good News Bible, which has sold in the millions. Each volume is informed by solid scholarship and the most u:-to-date research, yet each is biblically faithful and readily understandable to the general reader. Features include:

Introductory material highlighting authorship, dating, background information, and thematic emphases—plus a map

Full text of each Good News Bible book, with running commentary

Special end notes giving references for key words and concepts and providing suggestions for further reading

Full indexes for Scripture and Subjects/Persons/Places.

Series Editor W. Ward Gasque is Vice-Principal and Professor of New Testament at Regent College in Vancouver. A former editor-at-large for *Christianity Today*, he is the author of numerous articles and books and has edited *In God's Community: Studies in the Church and Its Ministry*, *Handbook of Biblical Prophecy*, *Apostolic History and the Gospel*, and *Scripture, Tradition, and Interpretation*. Dr. Gasque's major involvement is in the provision of theological resources and education for the laity.

Contents

Foreword

The Good News Bible Commentary Series

Although it does not appear on the standard best-seller lists, the Bible continues to outsell all other books. And in spite of growing secularism in the West, there are no signs that interest in its message is abating. Quite to the contrary, more and more men and women are turning to its pages for insight and guidance in the midst of the ever-increasing complexity of modern life.

This renewed interest in Scripture is found outside of, as well as in, the church. It is found among people in Asia and Africa as well as in Europe and North America; indeed, as one moves outside of the traditionally Christian countries, interest in the Bible seems to quicken. Believers associated with the traditional Catholic and Protestant churches manifest the same eagerness for the word that is found in the newer evangelical churches and fellowships.

Millions of individuals read the Bible daily for inspiration. Many of these lay Bible students join with others in small study groups in homes, office buildings, factories, and churches to discuss a passage of Scripture on a weekly basis. This small-group movement is one that seems certain to grow even more in the future, since leadership of nearly all churches is encouraging these groups, and they certainly seem to be filling a significant gap in people's lives. In addition, there is renewed concern for biblical preaching throughout the church. Congregations where systematic Bible teaching ranks high on the agenda seem to have no difficulty filling their pews, and "secular" men and women who have no particular interest in joining a church are often quite willing to join a nonthreatening, informal Bible discussion group in their neighborhood or place of work.

We wish to encourage and, indeed, strengthen this worldwide movement of lay Bible study by offering this new commentary series. Although we hope that pastors and teachers will find these volumes helpful in both understanding and communicating the Word of God, we do not write primarily for them. Our aim is, rather, to provide for the benefit of the ordinary Bible reader reliable guides to the books of the Bible, representing the best of contemporary scholarship presented in a form that does not require formal theological education to understand.

The conviction of editors and authors alike is that the Bible belongs to the people and not merely to the academy. The message of the Bible is too important to be locked up in erudite and esoteric essays and monographs written for the eyes of theological specialists. Although exact scholarship has its place in the service of Christ, those who share in the teaching office of the church have a responsibility to make the results of their research accessible to the Christian community at large. Thus, the Bible scholars who join in the presentation of this series write with these broader concerns in view.

A wide range of modern translations is available to the contemporary Bible student. We have chosen to use the Good News Bible (Today's English Version) as the basis of our series for three reasons. First, it has become the most widely used translation, both geographically and ecclesiastically. It is read wherever English is spoken and is immensely popular with people who speak English as a second language and among people who were not brought up in the church. In addition, it is endorsed by nearly every denominational group.

Second, the Good News Bible seeks to do what we are seeking to do in our comments, namely, translate the teaching of the Bible into terms that can be understood by the person who has not had a strong Christian background or formal theological education. Though its idiomatic and sometimes paraphrastic style has occasionally frustrated the scholar who is concerned with a minute examination of the original Greek and Hebrew words, there can be no question but that this translation makes the Scripture more accessible to the ordinary reader than any other English translation currently available.

Third, we wish to encourage group study of the Bible, particularly by people who have not yet become a part of the church but who are interested in investigating for themselves the claims of Christ. We believe that the Good News Bible is by far the best translation for group discussion. It is both accurate and fresh, free from jargon, and, above all, contemporary. No longer does the Bible seem like an ancient book, belonging more to the museum than to the modern metropolis. Rather, it is as comprehensible and up-to-date as the daily newspaper.

We have decided to print the full text of the Good News Bible—and we are grateful for the kind permission of the United Bible Societies to do this—in our commentary series. This takes up valuable space, but we believe that it will prove to be very convenient for those who make use of the commentary, since it will enable them to read it straight through like an ordinary book as well as use it for reference.

Each volume will contain an introductory chapter detailing the background of the book and its author, important themes, and other helpful information. Then, each section of the book will be expounded as a whole, accompanied by a series of notes on items in the text that need further clarification or more detailed explanation. Appended to the end of each volume will be a bibliographical guide for further study.

Our new series is offered with the prayer that it may be an instrument of authentic renewal and advancement in the worldwide Christian community and a means of commending the faith of the people who lived in biblical times and of those who seek to live by the Bible today.

W. WARD GASQUE

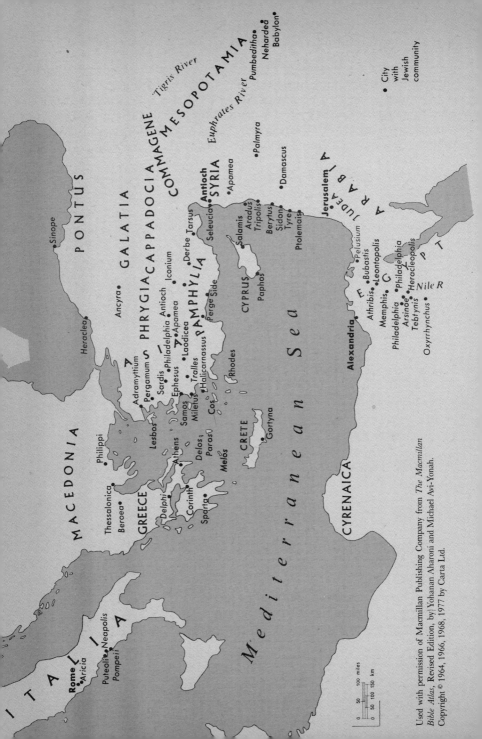

City with Jewish community

MESOPOTAMIA

Tigris River

COMMAGENE

Euphrates River

Nehardea
Pumbeditha
Babylon

Palmyra

CAPPADOCIA

SYRIA

Antioch
Apamea
Damascus

PONTUS

GALATIA

Sinope

Heraclea

Ancyra

PHRYGIA

Antioch
Iconium
Derbe
Tarsus
Seleucia

Apamea

Adramytium
Pergamum
Sardis
Philadelphia
Ephesus
Laodicea
Tralles
Miletus
Halicarnassus
Samos
Cos

PAMPHYLIA

Perge
Side

Aradus
Tripolis
Beryus
Sidon
Tyre
Ptolemais

Salamis

CYPRUS

Paphos

Rhodes

Jerusalem

JUDEA

ARABIA

Pelusium

Bubastis
Athribis
Leontopolis
Memphis
Philadelphia
Arsinoe
Tebtynis
Heracleopolis
Oxyrhynchus

Nile R

Alexandria

MACEDONIA

Philippi

Thessalonica
Beroea

GREECE

Delphi
Athens
Corinth
Sparta

Lesbos

Delos
Paros
Melos

CRETE

Gortyna

Mediterranean Sea

ITALIA

Rome
Aricia
Puteoli
Neapolis
Pompeii

CYRENAICA

Used with permission of Macmillan Publishing Company from *The Macmillan Bible Atlas*, Revised Edition, by Yohanan Aharoni and Michael Avi-Yonah. Copyright © 1964, 1966, 1968, 1977 by Carta Ltd.

0   50   100 miles
0 50 100 150 km

Acknowledgments

I want to thank my family, who have been my strong support, my encouragement, my best friends—Shirley, Anne, Jon, and Elizabeth. I also am grateful for the encouragement of my colleagues in ministry and the people of First Presbyterian Church of Berkeley, where it is my privilege to serve as pastor. I have dedicated this book to the men and women at New College Berkeley. Our experience together in this fellowship and common challenge have been a very exciting part of my life since those first organizational days of 1976. God has blessed us in this vision to relate biblical faith to our daily lives in the places where God has "posted" us.

Earl F. Palmer
Berkeley, California

Introduction

The year is A.D. 51, and a man named Paul, with his friends Silas and Timothy, has arrived in Corinth. Paul decides to write a letter to a group of young Christians in the principal metropolis of Macedonia.

The two brief letters he then wrote have been preserved, and we are able to read them almost two thousand years later. What Paul has to say is still fresh and challenging because the problems and issues that were the crises of the Thessalonian Christians are still active issues today. But more important than the issues, it is the faith of Paul that is as relevant now as it was in the first century. What Paul believed continues to be as startling and as good now when we meet it as it was in A.D. 51, in the world of Claudius, Seneca, Nero, and the rapidly growing band of Christians that were scattered throughout the cities of the Roman Empire.

These letters are teaching letters written from a teacher-pastor to an urban congregation of Christians. They are also personal letters written from a friend to friends. The letters are warm and human, clearheaded and salty.

However, 1 and 2 Thessalonians are not only the letters of Paul to a church; they are also documents within the whole witness that is called the Holy Bible. This means that these letters are a part of that inspired and faithful document of Old and New Testaments that God wants us to have. They are a part of the faithful witness to God's revelation of his character. Therefore I have read the letters not only with historical interest but in order to discover the living Center of the document, Jesus Christ. He is the Bible's center and the source of its authority.

But it was not always so for me. When I first began a serious reading of the Bible, I read it no differently from the way that I would read any book, and I still advise this approach to anyone who is starting out to investigate the Bible. Let the text speak for itself, and let its living Center win you to himself as this written witness to him makes sense and is confirmed in your own mind and experience. The texts of the Bible gain their authority in borrowed fashion from their center who is Jesus Christ himself. He is the one who must win each of us to himself.

I hope that this commentary will be a help to those of you who read it as an aid to your own entry into the letters of Paul to his friends. I have written a theological rather than a technical commentary, though I have attempted to put into focus the textual and technical problems as they arise.

We are considering in this commentary two letters, 1 and 2 Thessalonians, two very important books. They are generally regarded to be the earliest books of the New Testament, and for that reason they offer to us our initial look at the young church in the first-century Mediterranean world.[1] They show to us Paul[2] as he begins his distinguished career as a writer to congregations of believers; we are able to discover what issues and concerns first seize hold of the apostle's attention. •

But these letters are also important for what they teach to our lives and our time about discipleship some twenty centuries later. The great themes are just as relevant for Christians today as they were when they were first written about.

• Thessalonica, to which the letters are addressed, is an old city. In its earliest years it was called Therma. Its location was strategic, on the Via Egnatia, the major overland route from Italy to the East, and on the northeast corner of the Thermatic Gulf (the Gulf of Salonika). In 315 B.C. the city was named Thessalonica in honor of the half sister of Alexander the Great. In the year 146 B.C., after the Roman takeover of ancient Greece, this city was made capital of the Roman province of Macedonia. In 42 B.C. the city was further honored by being recognized as a "free city" by Rome. Because of the attempt of Rome to win Greek support, several cities of ancient Greece held this distinction (Athens and Sparta, for example, were also free cities); these cities were allowed more self-rule than other cities and were "exempt from all restrictions except the right to wage foreign or class war."[3] Luke gives a brief but very interesting narrative of the establishment of the Christian church in Thessalonica in the Book of Acts. He tells us that following Paul and Silas' imprisonment and release at Philippi (Acts 16:16–40), they left for the city of Thessalonica. "Paul and Silas traveled on through Amphipolis and Apollonia and came to Thessalonica, where there was a synagogue" (Acts 17:1).

We know from early documents and archaeological studies that Jewish synagogues existed in many of the cities of the Roman Empire. The word "synagogue" is transliterated into English from Greek and literally means "gathering" or "congregation." This word is used in both rabbinic literature and the New Testament in two ways: as a reference to the community of Jewish believers (e.g., Acts 6:9) and as a reference to the building in which the community met for worship (e.g., Matt. 4:23). As Jews scattered throughout the Mediterranean world, they established synagogues. Archaeologists have found evidence of a synagogue in Alexandria, Egypt, that dates from as early as 308 B.C. "A synagogue could be established wherever there were ten adult male Jews. . . . Judaism flourished in the Graeco-Roman world. Jews and their synagogues were to be found in all the principal cities."[4]

Luke tells us that Paul's practice was to attend the synagogue and share his faith in Jesus Christ as Messiah from within that setting: "According to his usual habit Paul went to the synagogue. There during three Sabbaths he held discussions with the people, quoting and explaining the Scriptures, and proving from them that the Messiah had to suffer and rise from death. 'This Jesus whom I announce to you,' Paul said, 'is the Messiah' " (Acts 17:2–3). Paul's message, according to Luke, is that the Messiah must suffer and that this suffering Messiah is in fact Jesus. Why this emphasis?

We know that Jewish messianic expectation by the time of the first century was that the Messiah would be like the conquering calf of Malachi who would trample the evildoers so that the arrogant would be like stubble to be burned (Malachi 4:1–6).[5] Israel thought of itself as the suffering servant of Isaiah 53; the Messiah, in contrast, was to be triumphant like the lion in the Intertestamental book 2 Esdras 12:31–34. "And as for the lion whom you saw rousing up out of the forest and roaring and speaking to the eagle and reproving him for his unrighteousness, and for all his words that you have heard, this is the Messiah whom the Most High has kept until the end of days, who will arise from the posterity of David, and will come and speak to them; he will denounce them for their ungodliness and for their wickedness, and will cast up before them their contemptuous dealings. For first he will set them living before his judgment seat, and when he has reproved them, then he will destroy them. But he will deliver in mercy the remnant of my people."

We catch the feel and energy of this expectation in the messianic speeches of John the Baptist (Luke 3:1–17). The Essenes, that band of strict Jews we have become more intimately acquainted with since the discovery of the Dead Sea Scrolls, were a pacifist movement in their early period; yet even this sect, by the time of the first century, conceived of the Messiah in Davidic naturalistic and conquering terms. "They cherished the text described as the *War of the Sons of Light against The Sons of Darkness*, which kept alive dreams of the day when the nations of the world should be successively destroyed in battle."[6]

But Paul has surprising good news to announce, and it tells of the Messiah who conquered evil and death by *taking upon himself* the fury of evil and the suffering and loneliness of death. He disarms these foes by absorbing their full intensity. Not only does the Messiah suffer real brokenness, but he conquers death with the real victory of resurrection. As for the enemies of righteousness, the Messiah identifies with the sinners and takes their place as well. This is Paul's message to the people in Thessalonica.

Luke tells of their mixed response: "Some of them were convinced and joined Paul and Silas; so did many of the leading women and a large group of Greeks who worshiped God. But the Jews were jealous and gathered some of the worthless loafers from the streets and formed a mob" (Acts 17:4–5).

Many people responded to Paul's message, including both Jews and Gentiles. Luke makes a special point of mentioning the fact that some of the city's prominent women accepted the message of Paul and Silas. Women played a vital role in the New Testament church, and this reference is one specific example of that fact.

The result of this acceptance is a riot. "They set the whole city in an uproar and attacked the home of a man called Jason, in an attempt to find Paul and Silas and bring them out to the people. But when they did not find them, they dragged Jason and some other believers before the city authorities" (Acts 17:5–6). Luke makes use of the word *politarchēs*, which is translated "authorities" in this paragraph. Only in this place in the New Testament does this unusual word appear. An ancient Roman letter discovered by archaeologists at Oxyrhynchus and dating from the early first century is addressed to one "Theophilus the Politarch." Also, a Roman arch has been discovered with inscriptions to "The Politarchs." This free city had its own city magistrates who bore this unusual title. Once again our chronicler of the early church, the Apostle Luke, must be given high marks for accuracy as a historian, even in side details.

Luke also tells us of the charges that are made against Paul and Silas and the new church at Thessalonica. Note the unintentional but unmistakable compliment that is paid to the early Christians and to their Lord. "These men have caused trouble everywhere! Now they have come to our city, and Jason has kept them in his house. They are all breaking the laws of the Emperor, saying that there is another king, whose name in Jesus" (Acts 17:6–7).

And so it was that in upheaval and turmoil the Christian church was born in one more capital city of the empire. "By men assembling here and there in the Holy Spirit there arises here and there a visible Christian congregation. . . . The first congregation was a visible group, which caused a visible public uproar. If the church has not this visibility then it is not the church."[7]

For the story to continue so that we may know what happens next in the life of this gathering of people, we must now turn to two letters that Paul wrote to these Christians soon after his arrival in Corinth. On the basis of the Acts 18:12 reference to the Roman official Gallio, whose dates at Corinth are certain, we are able to date this correspondence at about A.D. 51.

Notes

1. Some scholars, however, such as F. F. Bruce, W. Barclay, D. Guthrie, and R. P. Martin, believe that Paul's Letter to the Galatians was the first to be written (ca. A.D. 48-49).

2. Because of the New Testament Letters of this man and the narratives about him in Luke's Acts of the Apostles, we know more details about Paul than about any other first-century follower of Jesus Christ. Paul is also more self-expressive than other writers of the New Testament. He is to the New Testament what Jeremiah is to the Old Testament. Both of these writers take their readers into the full range of their emotional, spiritual, and intellectual journey. Whereas John is like Isaiah and remains more hidden, Paul shares himself in depth; we know Paul from his books better than we know John from his.

Paul is a citizen of three worlds, the Greek, the Jewish, and the Roman; he is fluent and at home within each of these worlds. He is a Roman citizen who is fully sophisticated in the pragmatic utilitarianism of the Roman lifestyle. He demonstrates a brilliant understanding of Greek thought and perspectives. His city is Tarsus, which was the city of Zeno, the founder of Stoicism, and at the time of Paul's childhood, it was, with its university and library, a center of Greek intellectualism. This remarkable city faced both to the East and to the West. "Wherein lay the peculiar suitability of Tarsus to educate and mold the mind of him who should in due time make the religion of the Jewish race intelligible to the Graeco-Roman world? . . . It lay in the fact that Tarsus was the city whose institutions best and most completely united the Oriental and the Western character" (William Ramsay, *The Cities of St. Paul* [London: Hodder & Stoughton, 1907], p. 88). But Paul is Jewish in his deepest intuitions and feelings. He writes in magnificent Greek, but he thinks in the rugged concrete mind-set of the Old Testament. Albert Schweitzer put it plainly and to the point in his 1912 study of Saint Paul: "The Apostle did not Hellenize Christianity. His conceptions are equally distinct from those of Greek philosophy and from those of the mystery-religions" (Albert Schweitzer, *Paul and His Interpreters* [New York: Schocken Books, 1974], p. 238). For a balanced introduction to Paul and the world in which he lived, see John Drane's life study (listed in For Further Reading).

3. Will Durant, *The Story of Civilization*, vol. 3 (New York: Simon & Schuster, 1944), p. 482.

4. Grant, p. 23

5. First-century messianic expectations by the Jewish people is a very widely discussed subject among scholars of the first-century period. See C. H. Dodd, *The Interpretation of the Fourth Gospel*; also Raymond E. Brown, *Gospel According to John*, Commentary Series Anchor Bible (New York: Doubleday, 1966), pp. 59 ff. Brown argues that John the Baptist's messianic expectation is for the "conquering lamb who will destroy evil in the world." John the Baptist was disappointed in the way of ministry that Jesus Christ chose for his Galilean ministry; there was a radical difference between the conqueror that

John expected and the Savior who would conquer by the way of the cross. John sent messengers to question Jesus (Luke 7) because he, like first-century Israel, expected a different kind of Messiah than God intended. This total surprise of Jewish expectations is evident in the Book of Acts sermons, which all emphasize that the Christ must suffer (Acts 17:2–3).

6. Rowley, p. 268.

7. Karl Barth, *Dogmatics in Outline* (New York: Harper & Row, 1959), p. 142.

Note: A list of the abbreviations used in the commentary is found at the end of the book (see p. 79). See also For Further Reading (p. 81); full bibliographical references for works referred to in short-form notes within the commentary are supplied there.

Real People in a Real Place

From Paul, Silas, and Timothy—
To the people of the church in Thessalonica, who belong to God the Father and the Lord Jesus Christ:
May grace and peace be yours.
1 Thessalonians 1:1

From Paul, Silas, and Timothy—
To the people of the church in Thessalonica, who belong to God our Father and the Lord Jesus Christ:
²May God our Father and the Lord Jesus Christ give you grace and peace.
2 Thessalonians 1:1–2

Paul begins both letters to his friends at Thessalonica in the formal style of first-century letter writing. We have many examples of first-century correspondence that follow the same essential design Paul employs in each of his letters. One such example is from a ship's captain named Irenaeus, to his brother, Apolinarius. Notice the similarity. "Irenaeus to Apolinarius his brother, my greetings. Continually I pray that you may be, even as I myself am in health" (quoted by William Barclay, *Commentary on the Letters of John and Jude*, p. 171). Paul identifies himself and his two companions **Silas** (Silvanus) and **Timothy**.

Paul writes to the gathering of the Thessalonians. *Ekklēsia* in classical Greek carries the meaning of "assembly" or "gathering." This word is used extensively in the New Testament, especially by Paul. It is here translated **people of the church**; the sense of the word is "gathering" or "congregation," not "building": the real people in a real place, Thessalonica. Paul writes to people **who belong to God the Father and the Lord Jesus Christ**. The congregation is defined by Paul in terms of not only its geographical location but also its relationship to God: the gathering at Thessalonica who belong to God who is Father and to Jesus Christ who is Lord.

Father is the intimate term that is used by Jesus Christ to describe both the nature of God's inner character and his relationship to God. Jesus makes use of this word in the prayer that he taught his disciples, "Our Father who art in Heaven . . ." (Matt. 6:8). Here the word Father is used to describe our relationship to God and his to us. Our Lord also uses this word to describe and express his own relationship to God. "Father, the hour has come . . ." (John 17:1). In both cases, this personal and direct word tells of the covenant relationship. Jesus further makes use of this word to uncover for us the inner character of God, for example, in the Parable of the Prodigal Son (Luke 15:11–32). Another example is in the Sermon on the Mount, where Jesus continues his teaching on prayer: "Or what man of you, if his son asks for bread, will give him a stone? . . . How much more will your Father who is in Heaven give good things to those who ask him!" (Matt. 7:9, 11). "Father" is the term that reveals God's care and love in these latter references.

The word **Lord** (*Kyrios*) is a common Greek word that means "master" or "owner." The verb form means literally "to rule." This title is given to Jesus Christ and expresses his authority and his reign; Paul does not qualify that reign. **Lord Jesus Christ** is the exact word order.

We are struck by the close relationship between God the Father and Jesus Christ the Lord, and within a few sentences we will hear Paul bear witness to the Holy Spirit.

Grace and peace used together will become a mark of the Apostle Paul in every letter that he will write. *Charis* ("grace") is a word that comes from the root *chara* ("joy") and carries the meaning "surprise gift." This word will take on special significance in Paul's writings as a part of his love vocabulary; he uses it as a word for God's powerful love. Note Romans 5:2 and Romans 5:20: "through whom also we have had our access by faith into this grace wherein we stand" and "where sin increased, grace abounded all the more." This surprise love gift has its origin in God the Father and in Jesus Christ the Lord.

The word **peace** is much richer as a Hebrew word than as a Greek word. The Greek word *eirēnē* is a mild and good word, but it carries little of the richness and depth of the Hebrew word *shalom*, which means "wholeness" and "health." It seems likely that Paul has drawn together the deep yearnings of both Greek world and Jewish world by means of this brief greeting. Any first-century Greek reader of Paul's letter would catch the similarity of Paul's *charis* to the ordinary Greek language greeting of *chairei*; Jewish readers would certainly read behind Paul's use of the word *eirēnē* the beautiful Jewish greeting of *shalom*. We have evidence that *shalom* was used in Jewish greetings just as *chara* was used in the greetings of the Greek world. For example, 2 Maccabees begins as follows: "The Jewish brethren in Jerusalem and those in the land of Judea, to their Jewish brethren in Egypt, greetings, and good peace" (2 Macc. 1:1). But both of these words are taken captive by Paul in 1 Thessalonians 1:2 and made dependent upon the God who is Father and Jesus Christ who is Lord.

A Chronology of the Life of Paul.

It is helpful to attempt to relate the Letters of Paul to the church at Thessalonica to the dates and events of his life. The following is a suggested outline of the chronology of his life, mission, and writing. It must be observed, however, that, although scholars are generally agreed on the main features of the outline, there is a great deal of guesswork involved in such a reconstruction.

ca. 5 B.C.–A.D. 5	The birth of Saul (Paul) in Tarsus
A.D. 33	The conversion of Paul
35	First postconversion visit to Jerusalem
35–46	Ministry in Cilicia and Syria
46	Second Jerusalem visit
47–48	First missionary journey: Cyprus and Galatia
49	Jerusalem Council
49–52	Second missionary journey: Asia Minor, Macedonia, and Achaia
51	First and Second Letters to the *Thessalonians*
51–52	In Corinth
52	Third visit to Jerusalem
52–55	In Ephesus
55–56	First and Second Letters to the *Corinthians*
55–57	In Macedonia, Illyricum, and Achaia
56	Letter to the *Galatians*
57	Letter to the *Romans*; Last visit to Jerusalem
57–59	Paul's arrest and imprisonment in Caesarea
59–60	Voyage to Rome and shipwreck
60–61	Under house arrest in Rome
	Letters to the *Colossians* and the *Ephesians*, Letter to *Philemon*, Letter to the *Philippians*
61–64	Further missionary activity in the East; Spain (?)
	First Letter to *Timothy*, Letter to *Titus*, Second Letter to *Timothy*
64	Martyrdom in Rome

Additional Notes

1 1:1; 2 1:1 / **Paul** is identified as the author of these letters. During the nineteenth century, certain scholars (K. Schrader and F. C. Baur) argued against the Pau-

line authorship of 1 and 2 Thessalonians. Their arguments primarily focused upon language choice and thematic material within the letters. Their arguments did not win scholarly support, and in fact, there is overwhelming consensus among New Testament interpreters that Saint Paul's authorship is validated by the text. The whole of the early church was also convinced of Paul's authorship. The scholar E. G. Selwyn has suggested that the similarities between these letters and 1 and 2 Peter might be due to the common link between these two men, in the person of Silvanus. An excellent survey of the authorship issue is found in the commentary by Ernest Best (pp. 22–28).

1 1:1; 2 1:2 / **Father** is the intentional, personal word used by Paul in this greeting, as it is also used by Jesus in the Our Father prayer of Matthew 6. This personal term was a point of controversy between Jesus and the Pharisees, according to John's Gospel (chapter 5). First-century Jewish rabbis had argued for a respectful restraint in the language of prayer toward God to such an extent that "there is no instance of the use of *Abba* ["Father"] as an address to God in all the extensive prayer literature of Judaism, whether in liturgical or in private prayers" (Joachim Jeremias, *New Testament Theology* [New York: Scribner, 1971], p. 65). The word **father** does, however, appear in early Old Testament prayer, as in the Song of Moses (Deut. 32:7). It is not correct to argue that Jesus had created a new word for human beings to use in the approach to God; instead Jesus, and now Paul, re-introduced the very old and personal term found in Moses.

1 1:1; 2 1:2 / The language of the Apostle Paul throughout his New Testament Letters reveals a writer who has a total grasp of Greek vocabulary; Paul understands and takes full advantage of the linguistic possibilities of the Greek language. His fascinating use of the word *charis* (**grace**) is an example of this skill and subtlety: he in effect captures a powerful and exciting word so that it becomes a part of his love vocabulary and expresses the surprise love gift of God to human beings. Throughout these two letters, as in all Paul's New Testament Letters, the reader is continually impressed by the wise and intriguing word choices that appear in the text. Many of these will be subjects of our later discussion.

Faith, Love, Hope

1 THESSALONIANS 1:2–10

We always thank God for you all and always mention you in our prayers. [3]For we remember before our God and Father how you put your faith into practice, how your love made you work so hard, and how your hope in our Lord Jesus Christ is firm. [4]Our brothers, we know that God loves you and has chosen you to be his own. [5]For we brought the Good News to you, not with words only, but also with power and the Holy Spirit, and with complete conviction of its truth. You know how we lived when we were with you; it was for your own good. [6]You imitated us and the Lord; and even though you suffered much, you received the message with the joy that comes from the Holy Spirit. [7]So you became an example to all believers in Macedonia and Achaia. [8]For not only did the message about the Lord go out from you throughout Macedonia and Achaia, but the news about your faith in God has gone everywhere. There is nothing, then, that we need to say. [9]All those people speak about how you received us when we visited you, and how you turned away from idols to God, to serve the true and living God [10]and to wait for his Son to come from heaven—his Son Jesus, whom he raised from death and who rescues us from God's anger that is coming.

1:2 / **In our prayers**: Paul prays for his friends at Thessalonica. If we read all of Paul's letters closely, we are impressed by how many people the apostle prayed for and for whom he was thankful. The word translated "we thank [God]," with which verse 2 begins, comes from the root word *charis*, "grace." It is *eucharistoumen* from which we get the word *Eucharist* for the act of thanksgiving at the Lord's Supper. The prefix *eu* in Greek means "good," and therefore, to express thanks means to express the good surprise gift toward another. Paul expresses this good surprise to God. There is a joyous quality in thanksgiving, and we sense that joy in Paul's use of this word; Paul is grateful to God for the Thessalonians. Thanksgiving and intercession go together in Paul. His word for prayer is the Greek word *proseuchomai*, "to pray toward"; because of the prefix *pros*, the emphasis of the word is on the Lord to whom Paul prays rather than on the art or skill of the act of prayer. In the Greek way of thinking, *euchomai*, from which we have the English word *evoke,* has within it the connotation of prayer as an art form, a religious act of skillful bargaining with the gods. But when the New Testament writers make use of this word for prayer, they add the prefix *pros*, which shifts the specific weight of the word away from the skill of evoking and toward the one to whom the prayer is directed. Prayer then becomes an amateur event, not the practiced, technical achievement of an expert.

1:2-3 / Your **faith** . . . **love** . . . **hope**. Paul now brings together three vital words that will play an important role in the story of Christian theology. Each word is supported in this sentence by another word. Notice what Paul says:

You put your faith into practice, literally, "your work of faith": The word that Paul employs here is *ergon*, which has the meaning of "work" in the sense of "deed" or "action," work as practical proof. This is the word Paul uses in Ephesians 4:12: "to equip the saints for the work of ministry." It has to do with the specific task or job that we have to do.

Paul is thankful and he prays, remembering the specific acts of faith—the work of faith—that he has seen in the lives of these Christians at Thessalonica. Paul here describes faith in the most practical terms possible. Faith is an event that can be seen because it produces a work. The Good News Bible translation is very helpful in this passage: There are marks of faith, and the Thessalonians have showed those marks.

Your love made you work so hard, literally, "labor of love." In this case Paul makes use of yet another Greek word, *kopos*, which means "difficulty," "toil," "hard work." It does not describe the task being done but instead the toil that it takes to do it.

The GNB rendering of this phrase catches this connotation: Love takes time; it happens over a span of time, and there is hard work at the core of it. Anyone who has loved a person through an estrangement, with its bitterness and anger, on to reconciliation knows why Paul has described love with a long-term kind of word like *kopos*. *Agapē* is the word that in English is "love," but this bland and colorless Greek word plays a very minor role in classical Greek vocabulary. *Agapē* has an uncertain etymology, "its meaning weak and variable . . . it is indeed striking that the substantive *agapē* is almost completely lacking in pre-biblical Greek" (*TDNT*, vol. 1, pp. 36–37). But Paul found this word when he read the Septuagint, the Greek translation of the Old Testament that had been produced sometime between 200 and 100 B.C. When Paul used the Old Testament, it was the Greek version that he usually referred to, though he can also make use of the Hebrew Bible and the Aramaic paraphrases. In the Greek Old Testament he found this word *agapē* being used by those translators to express God's love in the Old Testament, and that is how *agapē* came into the New Testament. Its rich meaning does not come out of classical Greek but from the Old Testament Hebrew word *ahab* and from its usage within the New Testament. The Bible thus becomes its own dictionary in the definition of its words, and Paul has begun that definition process.

Love is a dynamic word; it is an event that is happening not without toil. Within a sentence, Paul will describe the source of *agapē* as he reminds the Thessalonians that God is the one who loves first; it is his love that is prior to our labor of love. It is this very love that Dietrich Bonhoeffer describes as costly grace. "Such grace is costly because it calls us to follow Jesus Christ. . . . Above all, it is costly because it cost God the life of his Son: 'Ye were bought with a price,' and what has cost God much cannot be cheap for us" (Bonhoeffer, 1948, p. 37).

And how your hope in our Lord Jesus Christ is firm: The word for firm here, *hypomonē*, literally means "endurance." The verb form of this word means "to stay, hold out," "stand one's ground." It is the word Paul uses in 1 Corinthians 13:7, "Love *endures* all things." Paul is thankful because the Christians at Thessalonica have a hope that holds its ground. The word hope, *elpis*, means literally "expectation" or "prospect." There is a basic future orientation at the heart of the word, but the way Paul uses it is highly charged with present-tense meaning as well. These Christians are living in the present situation on the basis of their hope, that is, their expectation of and relationship with Jesus Christ as Lord. They endure in the present with a faith that has works and a love that is hard-working because they know that Jesus Christ reigns and will reign. That durability of their hope is what motivates and sustains them in the present. Notice that in Paul the hope is not at all portrayed in escapist language, as though **hope** were the word for future release from the trials of the present; Paul's choice of language in this vital passage is present tense and reality-oriented. For Paul, faith, hope, and love are at work here and now in our lives because of Jesus Christ.

1:4-8 / God loves you and has chosen you to be his own. The remainder of this first chapter in our text describes how these believers in Thessalonica first came to trust in the gospel. Paul begins with a clear affirmation that their faith was in response to God's prior decision on their behalf. Our faith does not trigger God's love toward us, but rather it is God's love and God's decision that precedes our faith and to which our faith responds. In this setting, the Apostle Paul teaches his readers about the authenticating ministry of the Holy Spirit. God is his own validation;

this is the doctrine of the Holy Spirit in the Bible. The mystery of the Holy Spirit has to do with the Triune nature of God—the mystery of divine fellowship within the very essence of God's nature—Father, Son, Holy Spirit. The ministry of the Holy Spirit has to do with assurance; he is the one who assures us of our belovedness. The Holy Spirit's power is thus the power of authentication. It has both a salty and a joyous side to it. The conviction of sin is its salty side, and the assurance of forgiveness to the repentant sinner is the joyous side. The Holy Spirit's power is also revealed in the ministry of companionship with Christians in their discipleship and life together as the church in the world. However, Paul has not drawn together in this Thessalonian text all of these threads of teaching concerning the Holy Spirit's ministry and person. In his letters to the Corinthians (chapter 12) and the Romans (chapter 8), Paul will more fully develop these themes. Here, Paul's main concern has been simply to state the central ministry, that of assurance. By the Holy Spirit God himself confirmed Paul's affirmation of the gospel, and the Thessalonians—men and women, Jews and Greeks—were convinced. Against great odds and in adversity, they believed; and Paul tells them that the joy they experienced in that conviction was a gift from the Holy Spirit, God himself.

As powerful as the confirmation of the Holy Spirit is, it does not cancel out the freedom of the person who hears the message of the gospel. This freedom theme is Paul's next concern as he writes to the church at Thessalonica.

1:9-10 / **You turned away from idols to God** is a "freedom sentence." Paul does not announce, "You were captured by God and stolen away from idols," because biblical faith is not seduction or the devastation of the human will by the almighty power of God. One of God's decisions is the decision that grants to us our real freedom. At the cosmic level of existence, that freedom decision by God allows for the existence of the devil too. God is so sure of himself that he can provide real freedom around himself, and in this first chapter of 1 Thessalonians, we see Paul sketch in that freedom theology at the very beginning of the New Testament.

Faith and love and hope are human action events that human beings decide about and are free to choose or to avoid. Paul insists upon this freedom. God does not overwhelm us, and therefore the ministry of the Holy Spirit is not an experience of the coercion of the human will by God, with or without mystically dramatic experiences. The ministry of the Holy Spirit is the ministry of assurance, but "no harm must be done to the critical choice" (Barth). We must beware of theological systems that lose this emphatic respect the gospel has for the freedom of God and the freedom of humanity.

In classical Greek, the word *idol, eidōlon,* means "shadow," "phantom." Paul now makes a fascinating observation about his Christian friends at Thessalonica. They **turned away from idols**. The idols collapsed; they were discredited as the shadows that they really are. Paul is describing a journey that these Christians experienced—a journey in which at some point they turned: They decided to turn away from the shadowy forms and designs with which they were holding their lives together. Were these people involved in Greco-Roman mystery cult religions, or the craft and trade guilds, which were religious in orientation? Or was it emperor worship? We know that capital cities in the Roman Empire were strong centers for this form of political-religious idolatry. Paul allows each reader to fill in the blank space. What matters to him is that these people turned away from the idols **to serve the true and living God**.

What a momentous event that "turn-away" is in itself! It is not salvation to leave the idols, but this is often one of the first steps–when a person knows what it is that he or she *doesn't* believe. It is like repentance that regrets sin and seeks to move away from sin. For some poeple this first move takes a great amount of time, and it may in itself occupy a large part of a human story. Many great novels and poems have been written about the discontent and the crises of this first move away from the gods that fail. Such literature may not document the move toward faith, hope, and love, but it tells of the move away from the shadows of despair.

T. S. Eliot's poems "The Love Song of J. Alfred Prufrock," "The Hollow Men," and "The Waste Land" are profoundly moving examples of an artist sketching into harsh focus the collapse of the idols. Joseph Conrad's *The Heart of Darkness* is another example of an author's relentless search into the hollow shell of man as his own God. When the idols fail, the Good News makes sense to us. "We cannot hear the last word until we have heard the next to the last word" (Bonhoeffer). The judgment of the idols is not the last word, it is the next to the last word; but that judgment must happen one way or another, and Paul recognizes the fact that it had happened in Thessalonica.

The idols are so impressive at first—"idols of gold and silver and bronze and stone and wood" (Rev. 9:20)—that it sometimes takes years before they are discredited. The gospel has a different sort of journey in a person's mind. As C. S. Lewis comments, "Its credibility does not lie in obviousness. Pessimism, optimism, pantheism, materialism, all have this 'obvious' attraction. Each is confirmed at the first glance by multitudes of facts! Later on, each meets insuperable obstacles. The doctrine of the incarnation . . . has little to say to the man who is still certain that everything is going to the dogs, or that everything is getting better and better, or that everything is God, or that everything is electricity. [The gospel's] hour comes when these wholesale creeds have begun to fail us" (*Miracles,* 1947, p. 157). The idols are not alive, and they are not true. John puts it in very basic fashion in the Revelation: "idols of gold and silver and bronze and stone and wood, which cannot either see or hear or walk" (Rev. 9:20; cf. Pss. 115:4-7, 135:15-17; Dan. 5:23).

The Thessalonians turned *toward* the true and living God; they discovered that he who made the ear can hear, he who made the eye can see, and he who made the mystery called the human being can speak for himself. We have made the shadows on the wall with our own hand, and we have called out the sounds, but God speaks for himself. He is truth and he is life.

Paul concludes this exciting summary with another reference to the hope that the Christians at Thessalonica have discovered for themselves the fact that it is Jesus Christ, the Son of God, who holds human history within the boundary of his Lordship (v. 10). As Christ stands at the center, so also he stands at the close of history as well. But Paul will have much more to say on this theme as his letter unfolds.

Additional Notes

1:4 / The term **brothers** is the plural form for *adelphos,* which in common Greek usage may properly be translated "brothers and sisters," since the term is used to connote close relatives, i.e., cousins, both female and male.

1:6 / The term **imitate** is the Greek *mimeomai,* a common word in both the theater and the classroom. It describes the way of learning that takes place from observation of a model or example, as when a skier learns ski technique by watching another skier and endeavoring to copy the example.

1:9-10 / Verses 9 and 10 offer a brief and powerful statement of the heart of the Christian faith. "This is one of the most important verses in the New Testament. It was written some twenty years after the resurrection, and it expresses in a few words much of the essence of Christianity" (Whiteley, p. 39). The sentence shows a twofold verbal movement, the turning away from idols and the turning toward God in active living. At the same time there is within the daily discipleship the lively sense of expectation of the return of Jesus Christ.

"Who delivers us from the wrath to come" (1:10c, RSV). The word for wrath (*orgē*) does carry the sense of anger, but William Neil notes C. H. Dodd's argument (1932, pp. 20 ff.) that Paul never uses "wrath" as referring "to an emotion or attitude of God towards man, but always as meaning 'an inevitable process of cause and effect in a moral universe' . . . not that God gets angry with us, but that God has created a moral universe in which retribution follows sin" (Neil, p. 32). Paul's point is that when the Thessalonians no longer trusted in the idols to grant meaning to their lives and turned toward Jesus Christ, they found the one who was able to break the vicious downward cycle of idolatry and despair. "Rather would he in His love save them from the sin that involves them in disaster. Paul, in line with this, therefore, holds up to the Thessalonians the only escape from the wrath to come, namely, Jesus, the Deliverer" (Neil, p. 33). See also "Wrath," *NBD*, p. 1341; "Anger, Wrath," in *NIDNTT* vol. 1, pp. 105–113; Leon Morris, *The Apostolic Preaching of Cross* (Grand Rapids: Eerdmans, 1956).

3

The Friends

1 THESSALONIANS 2:1–12

Our brothers, you yourselves know that our visit to you was not a failure. [2]You know how we had already been mistreated and insulted in Philippi before we came to you in Thessalonica. And even though there was much opposition, our God gave us courage to tell you the Good News that comes from him. [3]Our appeal to you is not based on error or impure motives, nor do we try to trick anyone. [4]Instead, we always speak as God wants us to, because he has judged us worthy to be entrusted with the Good News. We do not try to please men, but to please God, who tests our motives. [5]You know very well that we did not come to you with flattering talk, nor did we use words to cover up greed—God is our witness! [6]We did not try to get praise from anyone, either from you or from others, [7]even though as apostles of Christ we could have made demands on you. But we were gentle when we were with you, like a mother[a] taking care of her children. [8]Because of our love for you we were ready to share with you not only the Good News from God but even our own lives. You were so dear to us! [9]Surely you remember, our brothers, how we worked and toiled! We worked day and night so that we would not be any trouble to you as we preached to you the Good News from God.

[10]You are our witnesses, and so is God, that our conduct toward you who believe was pure, right, and without fault. [11]You know that we treated each one of you just as a father treats his own children. [12]We encouraged you, we comforted you, and we kept urging you to live the kind of life that pleases God, who calls you to share in his own Kingdom and glory.

a. We were gentle when we were with you, like a mother; *some manuscripts have* we were like children when we were with you; we were like a mother.

Paul's Letter to the Thessalonians contains a very long personal narrative (1:5–3:13). Paul reminds his Christian friends in Thessalonica of the experience they and he and Silas, and later Timothy, shared. As we seek to interpret it, we must ask why Paul sketches with such detail this story that they already know. It is their story, and Paul retells it to them. It is also Paul's story, the account of his own journey, his motivations and goals, and his style of life when he was with the church in its critical founding months. In my view, Paul has a very definite pastoral and theological goal in mind during this part of the letter.

Something has happened at Thessalonica in the church and among the Christians that makes it important for them to begin once again at their origins. He thinks through the early experiences with them like a psychotherapist who carefully draws out from a patient the story of the journey that has taken place in the person's life. In this case it is Paul who remembers the details, but the effect of this passage for the Thessalonians is to remind them of key ingredients in their early experience. If Paul is accurate in his narration, then he will draw his readers into vital rediscovery of parts of their spiritual journey that they may have forgotten.

But how does narrative material such as that in 2:5–3:13 become theologically significant for the twentieth-century reader, for the reader who is not a participant in the story but looks in as an observer? For later readers, such material is a case history from which we learn as we discover similarities to our own situation and as we discover principles and truths that underlay particular experiences of the Thessalonian Christians.

2:1 / **Our brothers**: The plural of *adelphos,* "brother," which Paul makes use of twenty-one times in 1 and 2 Thessalonians, is a warm and affectionate term and should properly be translated "brothers and sisters" in each instance, since the word appears in the plural. There are numerous examples of this intent in the word's use, both in classical Greek and in New Testament usage.

2:2 / **Our God gave us courage to tell you the Good News that comes from him**. The exact phrase in Greek is "the Good News of God." The form of the word *theos* ("God") is possessive; that is to say, "the gospel that belongs to God," or "the gospel that has its origin in God." Several times in this narrative, Paul will make use of this phrase "Good News [gospel] of God"; it is a very important phrase for his theology.

Good news, *euangelion*, is a Greek word made up of two parts: the prefix *eu*, which means "good," and the word *angelion*, which means "message." It was not a religious word in the Greek of Paul's day but certainly an exciting, electrifying word. The word is used in the Greek translation of the Old Testament, however, for the "good tidings" concerning a new era in world history, an era of peace and salvation. "In the mouth of his messengers, God himself speaks; he speaks and it is accomplished; he commands and it is done" (NIDNTT, vol. 2, p. 109). The word, of course, is a claim, and it only has real substance and meaning if the claim is true. Therefore, Paul immediately assigns the Good News to its source: God. The Good News is good because its source is good. God backs up this good message. Paul reminds his brothers and sisters at Thessalonica that what they heard from Paul and Silas was the Good

News that comes from God—not from Paul or from any other temporary source, but from the Source who sustains everything.

2:3–6 / You know very well that we did not come to you with flattering talk . . . to cover up greed . . . to get praise: Paul now asks his readers to recall their own experience of his ministry in their city. Two things are happening together in this part of Paul's recap of the Thessalonica experience. First, his readers are reminded of the pattern of life and deportment of Paul and Silas during those early months at the beginning of the Thessalonian's Christian pilgrimage. Secondly, Paul reminds his friends in Thessalonica of how they became followers of Christ in those early days.

It is clear that they did not become Christians because of "flattery." The word Paul uses here is *kolakia*, which in classical Greek carries the idea of enticement. It is not used in any other place in the New Testament, though it has wide usage in classical Greek, usually in the negative sense of "tortuous methods by which one [person] seeks to gain influence over another" (MM, p. 352). Paul reminds the Thessalonian Christians that they were not enticed or deceived into becoming Christians. No "heavenly deception" was employed to win them over to the way of discipleship. Paul wants them to remember this fact now in the place which they now occupy. The implication is that Paul's message did not require the enticements of false promises or interpersonal relationships; it was compelling because of its inner integrity and truth.

It is clear that they did not become Christians because of money, just as Paul did not announce the Good News for money. It is also clear that their faith was not won by promises of glory, nor did Paul preach in order to win glory for himself. *Doxa* is the word here translated "praise" and in the RSV, "glory." The word literally means "brightness," "splendor," "radiance"; hence it carries the meaning of "fame," "renown," "honor." The fact is, at Thessalonica, as the Christians there know, Jason and the other Christians, as well as Paul and Silas, were exposed to great danger as a reward for the breakout of the gospel in the lives of people.

2:7–9 / But we were gentle when we were with you, like a mother taking care of her children. Because of our love for you we were ready to share with you not only the Good News from God but even our own lives. The literary construction of this sentence is quite remarkable. It is the language of the nursery. A very rare word, *homeiromai*, is used by Paul to explain his love for the Thessalonians. "So dear to us" in the GNB, it is translated in the RSV "being affectionately desirous." It is a word that, according to Westcott and Hort in their New Testament text, has a connection to the idea of breathing. The Septuagint (the pre-Christian Greek translation of the Old Testament) makes one use of the word, in Job 3:21, where it has the sense of "longing." Milligan agrees with the view that this word is used "as a term of endearment" (MM, p. 22). Though the word choices by Paul are quite unusual, certainly the warmth of the total passage is unmistakable.

Paul not only told the truth of the Good News to the people in this city, he shared his own life with them. A person who wants to teach small children cannot simply announce a great theory and doctrine but must spend the time to become fully involved with the pupils, or else very little real communication will occur. It takes time to teach in the nursery; this was Paul's style.

2:10–12 / **We encouraged you, we comforted you, and we kept urging you to live the kind of life that pleases God**: The word translated *comforted* here is the word *parakaleō*, a word Paul makes extensive use of throughout his letters. The word means "to come alongside" and therefore is translated by "encourage" or "comfort" in the English text of the New Testament. In John's Gospel the noun form is the word used to refer to the Holy Spirit—the one who comes alongside to help.

They have been reminded that they were won to and by the gospel of God. It was this true and alive eternal positive that won them away from the idols of the empire. They also now remember that they were won by the experience of love from other human beings who came alongside of them, Paul and Silas. It was not an ideological transaction but a deeply personal conversion that they experienced—not words alone but words and life united.

Additional Notes

2:1 / **Our brothers**: Luke makes the observation, both in connection with the church at Thessalonica and in Paul's experience in Athens, that women were leaders in the life of the New Testament church. In the Letters to the Philippians, two of the women in that church are of such significance that their controversy threatens to disrupt the whole fellowship; therefore, Paul singles out Euodia and Syntyche for special attention (Phil. 4). The early church was quite different from the synagogue in this regard. In the synagogue the role of women was downgraded by both their physical position in the location of worship and the very meager part they were permitted to take in the life of the synagogue. But we have unmistakable evidence in the Book of Acts (in the narratives about the founding of the church at Thessalonica, Athens, and Corinth) that women took a key role in the total life of the fellowship of the early Christians. Just as women are crucial in the resurrection narratives, so throughout the founding of the first-century church the women as much as the men are the prophets of this mighty act of God. It is fitting that Peter should quote Joel's prophecy at the moment of the church's birth on the day of Pentecost: "Your young men and your young women shall prophesy." This is in fact what happens as the Christian church is born throughout the Mediterranean world.

Our visit to you: The visit to Thessalonica is narrated by Luke in Acts 17. Paul notes the success of that visit, even though there was considerable hardship and persecution at Thessalonica.

2:7 / Paul's use of the term *apostles* in 1 Thessalonians and his extensive defense of the word in Galatians points up its importance in the early church. The term "meant at the time of Paul's writing a cohesive group . . . situated in or near Jerusalem . . . who based their accreditation on the post resurrection appearance of Jesus" (Rudolph Schnackenburg, "Apostles Before and During Paul's Time," *Apostolic History and the Gospel*, ed. W. Ward Gasque and Ralph P. Martin [Grand Rapids: Eerdmans, 1970], p. 291). Paul is a missionary apostle and he is conscious of the fact that he is "an active participant in the larger group of apostles" (p. 295). "It makes no sense to play the 'charismatic' and 'institutional' concepts of an Apostle one against the other. Rather the concept of an Apostle, at the beginning, was not carefully defined. During this period Paul had to be active as an Apostle and needed to succeed against those who contested his apostleship. He faced all the requirements, the ones which came from the 'apostles before him' in Jerusalem, as well as those which were presented by apostles during his time, and in this he clarified his own understanding of his ministry as an apostle" (pp. 302, 303).

4

Hardships

1 THESSALONIANS 2:13–20

And there is another reason why we always give thanks to God. When we brought you God's message, you heard it and accepted it, not as man's message but as God's message, which indeed it is. For God is at work in you who believe. ¹⁴Our brothers, the same things happened to you that happened to the churches of God in Judea, to the people there who belong to Christ Jesus. You suffered the same persecutions from your own countrymen that they suffered from the Jews, ¹⁵who killed the Lord Jesus and the prophets, and persecuted us. How displeasing they are to God! How hostile they are to everyone! ¹⁶They even tried to stop us from preaching to the Gentiles the message that would bring them salvation. In this way they have completed the full total of the sins they have always committed. And now God's anger has at last come down on them!

¹⁷As for us, brothers, when we were separated from you for a little while—not in our thoughts, of course, but only in body—how we missed you and how hard we tried to see you again! ¹⁸We wanted to return to you. I myself tried to go back more than once, but Satan would not let us. ¹⁹After all, it is you—you, no less than others!—who are our hope, our joy, and our reason for boasting of our victory in the presence of our Lord Jesus when he comes. ²⁰Indeed, you are our pride and our joy!

2:13 / Paul continues the narration of his own experience with the Christians at Thessalonica. He reminds them of a central theological fact about their response to the message of Paul and Silas. The message that they received from Paul was the "Good News of God," received **not as man's message but as God's message, which indeed it is**. Paul wants to make this distinction very clear. We are strongly reminded by the following paragraph of Paul's Letter to the Galatians, also one of the earliest of Paul's letters. "I would have you know, brethren, that the Gospel which was preached by me is not man's Gospel" (Gal. 1:11, RSV). There are so many "gospels" in the world; there are many counterfeit gospels that are in competition for the minds and the hearts of the people. Paul is aware of this fact, and he is also aware of the continuing pressure upon the Christians at Thessalonica as they are daily confronted with these various "gospels." Therefore, he journeys with them through the early formative days of their discovery of the gospel of Jesus Christ. The exciting fact is that when the Thessalonians received the message from Paul and Silas, their faith was validated by the inner work of God within their lives. **For God is at work in you who believe**: The word for **work** here is the word *energeia*, which is the root *erg* that we met earlier, in 1:3, where Paul spoke of "your work of faith" (RSV), "put your faith into practice" (GNB). In that case the word *ergon* means "work" in the sense of a specific work or event. Now the word *energeia* is used in the sense of "energy," "action," "powerful effect." Paul's point is that as the Thessalonians believed the message of the gospel, faith in the truth on their part was matched by God's powerful, authenticating, and life-changing action in their lives. This is no small thing that happened at Thessalonica, and Paul wants to be certain that the Christians in that city recognize what really happened. It was not simply a matter of their agreement with an argument made by Paul; it was not his eloquence that confirmed in them the truth of their experience of the gospel of God. It was God himself who verified himself.

The theology expressed here is vitally important for the twentieth-century church. Evangelists and apologists need to know that the task of authenticating the message is a task that only God himself is able to perform. Christians also need to know that the message we are to share with our generation is *God's* message; we do not create that message or control it. Christians need to remember that God is powerfully at work in the lives of those who believe the Good News.

2:14–16 / You suffered the same persecutions: Paul continues to encourage the Christians at Thessalonica, carefully journeying with them through their experiences of hardship and persecution as a result of their faith in Jesus Christ. He decides to place the persecution experiences of the Thessalonian Christians in a larger context. He points out to these friends that as they suffer, so have other brothers and sisters suffered for their faith in Jesus Christ. He speaks of the Christians in Judea (Jerusalem); they are persecuted by people in their city just as the Thessalonians are suffering persecution from people in their city.

The worst form of suffering is that which happens in isolation and loneliness. Paul's purpose is therefore pastoral as he helps the young Christians in a difficult place to see that they are not alone, they experience their own crises and their own difficult situation in fellowship with other Christians in another place.

From the Jews: Paul's disappointment with his own cultural and national heritage now comes to the surface in a few angry sentences. His portrayal is apparently total and final in its negative assessment of the

Jews who displease God. Paul speaks of God's anger which has **at last come down on them**. It would appear from these sentences that the Apostle Paul has said everything that he intends to say about the Jews. But Paul has very much more to say, and some years later he will write three decisive chapters about the Jews in his greatest letter (Rom. 9, 10, and 11). These three chapters will put Paul's teaching into the larger context that such a matter, namely, the relationship of the Jews to God's promises and the fulfillment of that promise in Jesus Christ, deserves. Therefore, when we read this brief passage in 1 Thessalonians 2:14-16, it is important not to draw hasty conclusions apart from Paul's later discussion.

2:17-20 / The second chapter concludes with Paul's affectionate words to his friends. He wants them to know how much they mean to him personally. They are his **hope** and his **joy**. These sentences are like the sentences parents write to their children, or children to their parents. The Christian fellowship is like a family, and Paul uses family language throughout this whole section. When a youngster is growing up, it is essential for that child to know that the family cannot get along without him or her. Each child is essential to the family, not expendable. We as a family need each of our children, or we are not complete. (Most youngsters who feel insecure are insecure basically because they somehow do not sense their own importance. Parents would do well to follow Paul's lead in letting their children know how really great they are.) Very often our children are told of their mistakes and of the serious and expensive responsibility they pose for the family, but what of their glory and their joy? We should remind our children that they are our **pride** ("glory," *doxa* is the word used) and **joy** (v. 20).

The same principle is true for the relationship of Christians in the extended family that is the church. The substantial affirmation that the Thessalonian Christians are experiencing from Paul should be a model for the Christian church today. The best cure for false pride is genuine affirmation. Proud people are usually covering up a hollowness on the inside, an inner inadequacy; but when people really know how important they are to other people and to their happiness, the result is not sinful pride but expansive generosity.

Paul has described the "weight of glory" (2 Cor. 4:17) to the Christians at Thessalonica. What we must not miss in this celebrative statement of Paul is that the coming of Jesus Christ is not only a joyous expectation for Paul himself but also for the Christians at Thessalonica.

If they are a reason for Paul's joy, then they are themselves set free to rejoice. I can think of nothing more liberating and self-affirming than what Paul has shared with his friends in these sentences. Think of how much the gospel shows us about ourselves! It shows us our sinfulness with vivid, inescapable clarity, but the gospel shows to us our belovedness with the same brilliant clarity. We need both to have the whole picture. We remember the idols, but we have our eyes on Christ.

Additional Notes

2:14-15 / What does the term **the Jews** mean to Paul? From Acts we observe that Paul's anger has been stirred toward certain Jews who opposed his affirmation of the gospel. Paul's feelings on this subject will continue to intensify during his missionary journey, to such a point that at Corinth (Acts 18) he will impulsively announce that he has no further plans to bear witness to the Jews. But one sentence further on, the president of the synagogue at Corinth trusts in the gospel, so that Paul's pessimistic feelings about his own people are greatly altered. Paul here is referring to the leaders of Palestinian Judaism in his day, who had rejected the Good News when it was proclaimed by Jesus and had continued to refuse to believe. He is not referring to *all* Jews—since he himself was a Jew, as were a great many of the earliest Christians—certainly not to Jews of a later historical period. Paul was not anti-Semitic in his thinking, nor should any of his modern-day spiritual descendants be.

2:19 / **Reason for boasting of our victory** is translated "crown of pride" in Moffatt and "crown of boasting" in RSV. It is not a reference to royalty, but rather Paul probably has in mind the "victors' laurel wreath awarded at athletic games or a garland worn at some festive occasion" (Neil, p. 59). See article on "Crown" in ISBE, vol. 2, pp. 831–32; also, NIDNTT, vol. 1, pp. 405–406. Other references in Paul to "crown, prize" (stephanos) are 1 Cor. 9:24, Phil. 4:1, and 2 Tim. 4:8.

5

The Strategy of Paul

1 THESSALONIANS 3:1–13

Finally, we could not bear it any longer. So we decided to stay on alone in Athens ²while we sent Timothy, our brother who works with us for God in preaching the Good News about Christ. We sent him to strengthen you and help your faith, ³so that none of you should turn back because of these persecutions. You yourselves know that such persecutions are part of God's will for us. ⁴For while we were still with you, we told you ahead of time that we were going to be persecuted; and as you well know, that is exactly what happened. ⁵That is why I had to send Timothy. I could not bear it any longer, so I sent him to find out about your faith. Surely it could not be that the Devil had tempted you and all our work had been for nothing!

⁶Now Timothy has come back, and he has brought us the welcome news about your faith and love. He has told us that you always think well of us and that you want to see us just as much as we want to see you. ⁷So, in all our trouble and suffering we have been encouraged about you, brothers. It was your faith that encouraged us, ⁸because now we really live if you stand firm in your life in union with the Lord. ⁹Now we can give thanks to our God for you. We thank him for the joy we have in his presence because of you. ¹⁰Day and night we ask him with all our heart to let us see you personally and supply what is needed in your faith.

¹¹May our God and Father himself and our Lord Jesus prepare the way for us to come to you! ¹²May the Lord make your love for one another and for all people grow more and more and become as great as our love for you. ¹³In this way he will strengthen you, and you will be perfect and holy in the presence of our God and Father when our Lord Jesus comes with all who belong to him.[b]

b. all who belong to him; *or* all his angels.

3:1–5 / Finally . . . we sent Timothy. Timothy first appears in Acts 16:1 during Paul's visit to Lystra. "A disciple was there, named Timothy, the son of a Jewish woman who was a believer; but his father was a Greek." Timothy is listed as a companion of Paul and Silas during the journey of Acts 16; however, there is no mention of his name in Acts 16:19–40 during the imprisonment of Paul and Silas at Philippi, nor of the Apostle Timothy's subsequent visit to Thessalonica (Acts 17:1–9). We meet his name in the text again in Berea (Acts 17:14). We cannot conclude absolutely that Timothy was not present with Paul and Silas during the visit at Thessalonica; however, since his name is omitted in that narrative, this is possible. Certainly Timothy finally came to Thessalonica when Paul sent him to the young church from Athens. The way Paul carefully describes his relationship with Timothy is an argument in favor of the view that Timothy was not present during the original visit of Paul and Silas.

3:6–10 / Paul also expresses his strong desire to personally visit the Christians at Thessalonica (vv. 10–11). There can be no question that Paul loves these people very much and that he prays for them and wants to be personally with them. They have suffered together, and out of that shared experience of crisis they have developed a bond of unshakable fellowship. Dietrich Bonhoeffer, a twentieth-century disciple, wrote with great feeling of that same quality of fellowship, which he experienced in a prison camp. "The air that we breathe is so polluted by mistrust that it almost chokes us. But where we have broken through the layer of mistrust we have been able to discover a confidence hitherto undreamed of. Where we trust, we have learnt to put our very lives into the hands of others . . . we have learnt never to trust a scoundrel an inch, but to give ourselves to the trustworthy without reserve" (*Letters and Papers from Prison*, 1953, p. 11).

Timothy is such a friend; he has power to be trustworthy under pressure, and Paul affirms that trustworthiness of Timothy to the Thessalonians. His goal is to keep and nourish the ties that exist between the young church at Thessalonica and the Apostle and his companions. In this passage it is Timothy who is especially noted as the one who is keeping that linkage growing and current.

It is important to observe that though Paul's strategy of ministry is highly mobile he never abandons the churches of his pilgrimage. Paul at Athens and at Corinth still feels obligated to the Christians at Galatia and Thessalonica. This concern will mark Paul's whole ministry. Paul feels a sense of social concern for the Christians he met at Jerusalem, and though he is immersed in the concerns of the gentile churches of southern Europe, he will nevertheless work hard at taking up an offering for the physical needs of the church at Jerusalem. Paul is a global Christian, and the international, cross-cultural style of Paul has left its indelible mark upon biblical Christianity. Because the apostle had this deliberate strategy of connectionalism, he needed to keep up a lively correspondence with the churches. For the same reason, Paul needed to continually train colleagues in faith who would be able to encourage the young churches. Timothy is one of those Christians who is being trained in faith by the apostle.

Paul's strategy takes risks with the newly established churches. And it leans heavily upon the conviction that the Holy Spirit is able to preserve the churches and strengthen the growing leadership in the churches as that leadership grows by taking on responsibility and ministry. It is this confidence of Paul that dominates the third chapter. He is confident that the Thessalonians are able and willing to learn from Timothy (v. 2); he is confident of the dynamic and growing quality of their faith (vv. 7–10); and he is praying for their growth in love and holiness (vv. 12–13)—these final two virtues are not the object of Paul's exhortation but of his prayer. Both love and holiness are gifts from God within which we grow. God himself is the source of love and holiness. It is on this note that Paul concludes this very personal opening section of the letter.

Additional Notes

3:1 / **Athens**: The Book of Acts tells of Paul's journey from Thessalonica to Berea and then to **Athens**, where Paul delivered his most famous New Testament sermon (Acts 17:16–31).

3:2 / **Timothy**: This young man was Paul's companion and close friend throughout Paul's second and third missionary journeys. We meet him first in Acts 16:1. "He appears to have been commissioned and commended to the ministry of the gospel by the elders of the church at Lystra" (F. F. Bruce, *Book of Acts* [Grand Rapids: Eerdmans, 1954], p. 322). It is Timothy who will be the recipient of Paul's final Letter in the New Testament canon (2 Timothy, written about A.D. 64 or 65).

3:13 / The word **holy** (*hagios*) is united to the word "love" (*agapē*) in 12. "Love and holiness are not in this context two virtues among other virtues but are umbrella words for the whole of Christian activity" (Best, p. 191). Paul goes beyond making an appeal to the Thessalonians in favor of their determination toward love and holiness. This verse is, rather, a prayer on their behalf that they will receive love and holy blamelessness as a gift from God that is now dynamically at work within their lives.

6

Christian Discipleship and Christian Marriage

Finally, our brothers, you learned from us how you should live in order to please God. This is, of course, the way you have been living. And now we beg and urge you in the name of the Lord Jesus to do even more. ²For you know the instructions we gave you by the authority of the Lord Jesus. ³God wants you to be holy and completely free from sexual immorality. ⁴Each of you men should know how to live with his wifeᶜ in a holy and honorable way, ⁵not with a lustful desire, like the heathen who do not know God. ⁶In this matter, then, no man should do wrong to his fellow Christian or take advantage of him. We have told you this before, and we strongly warned you that the Lord will punish those who do that. ⁷God did not call us to live in immorality, but in holiness. ⁸So then, whoever rejects this teaching is not rejecting man, but God, who gives you his Holy Spirit.

c. live with his wife; *or* control his body.

4:1-2 / **You learned from us how you should live**: Paul now writes directly and clearly to his friends. He calls them to live out in their daily lives what they learned from him concerning Jesus Christ their Lord. Paul insists that they have their instructions already. The GNB puts it, **you know the instructions we gave you by the authority of the Lord Jesus**. Paul makes use of a military word, *parangellō*. The verb form of this word means " to give orders or commands," as, for example, in Acts 1:4: "He *charged* them not to depart from Jerusalem." The noun form is used in this 1 Thessalonians 4:2 passage and in only three other places in the New Testament: 1 Timothy 1:18 (where it is translated "this *charge* I commit to you"), Acts 16:24 (where it describes the Phillippian jailer: "having received this *charge*, he put them into the inner prision"), and Acts 5:28 (where it appears in another famous setting: "we strictly *charged* you not to teach"). From these citations we see the strong force of this word. Paul now uses *parangellō* with his friends so that they will feel the importance of the imperative. They have marching orders.

4:3 / God wants you to be holy and completely free from sexual immorality. The first three words in Greek are literally "This is the will of God." The word *thelēma* is a noun that comes from the verb root *thelō*, which means "to will" in the sense of "purpose," "resolve," "design." Paul makes extensive use of this word and uses it always in the sense of purpose. "This is the purpose of God for you." The word translated *holy* in the GNB and "sanctification" in the RSV is the word *hagiasmos*, "the process of being made or becoming holy" from the word *hagios* ("holy"). "Holiness" in the Bible always has to do with the character and the presence of God. It is a relationship word in the way Paul makes use of it here. It is God's will that Christians should be drawn into God's holy presence and to be participants in the holy character of God. This is what it means to grow as a Christian. We are to experience God's character at work in a Christian. We are to experience God's character at work in our daily lives; we are to stay close to him and loyal to his purpose for our lives.

The GNB translates the word *porneia* "sexual immorality." The RSV translates it "unchastity." In classical Greek the word meant literally "to sell," hence it came to mean a "person for hire." The word conveyed the idea of harlotry and every kind of unlawful sexual intercourse when it was used by the Septuagint translators and New Testament writers. It is also used in the New Testament in a figurative sense to refer to idolatry and moral confusion, as, for example, in Revelation 18:3. The Christians at Thessalonica are challenged not to distort or twist the meaning of their lives, to sell out what they are or their personal relationships in a cheap and degrading way.

4:4–5 / Each of you men should know how to live with his wife. This sentence has been a problematic sentence for translators and interpreters because of Paul's use of the word *skeuos*, which literally means "vessel" (GNB: **wife**).

Early interpreters concluded that Paul meant "body." This interpretation lies behind the translations of the Jerusalem Bible and the New International Version. Milligan and Calvin also interpreted *skeuos* in this way. This understanding would suggest that what Paul is teaching is that Christians should not be lustful in the way they approach their own bodies. Saint Augustine rejected this interpretation. He held that by the use of the word "vessel" Paul's intended meaning was "wife," not "body." We have evidence to support Augustine in this interpretation in ancient rabbinic writings in which "to use as a vessel" and "to make one's vessel" are euphemisms for having sexual intercourse (see MM, p. 48–49; *TDNT*, vol. 7, pp. 361–62, 365–67). Also, in 1 Peter 3:7 the wife and the husband are both referred to as "vessels." Moffatt, in his translation, favors the word "wife" as does the RSV and the GNB. It seems awkward and unlikely that Paul would speak of a man "acquiring" his own body or living with his own body in holiness and honor and not harming his neighbor in this matter. The vocabulary and total context, in my view, favors Augustine's interpretation. Paul is here putting into focus the most intimate of all human relationships.

The most exhaustive discussion of this remarkable word choice by Paul is in the celebrated *Theological Dictionary of the New Testament*, edited by Gerhard Kittel. Professor Maurer concludes his philological study in that volume as follows: "In the light of this linguistic development, which would be possible for any bilingual Jew and not just for Paul alone, the most probable interpretation of 1 Thessalonians 4:3 is . . . : 'For this is the will of God, even your sanctification, that you keep yourselves from fornication, that every one of you know how to hold his own vessel in sanctification and honor (i.e., live with his wife in sanctification and honor), not in passionate lust like the Gentiles who know not God.' " Maurer concludes, "Material as well as linguistic considerations favor 'wife' rather than 'body' in interpretation of I Thessalonians 4:4" (*TDNT*, vol. 7, pp. 366–67).

Not with a lustful desire: The idea here is an accurate description of the interpersonal atmosphere of the first century. Paul teaches that the relationship of marriage is affected by our relationship with God. Because we know God, our most intimate relationship is profoundly molded and influenced. *Epithumia* (GNB: **lustful desire**) is a very brutal word. It is interesting that the root word *thumos* means "strong anger" or "rage." How quickly intense desire tumbles into the fierce rage of runaway desire! It is this overwhelming egotism that Paul warns against. He is not discounting meaningful desire, a vital ingredient in marriage (1 Cor. 7:36, "if his passions are strong, . . . let them marry"). He is arguing against runaway desire that uses people and destroys relationships. Marriage is a personal and private relationship of two people, but Paul has brought even this intimate personal relationship into the larger wholeness of the gospel of God. Marriage benefits when this holy intervention takes place.

4:6 / Paul warns his friends at Thessalonica about the seriousness of this matter. The harsh word *ekdikos* (lit., "avenger") is now used by Paul. This is the same root word that Paul used in Romans 12:19, "Vengeance is mine, I will repay, says the Lord."

Paul's point is clear. The Christian who lives in the first century is not to model his or her life on the standards that prevail in the cities of the Roman world. The sexual exploitation of women and youth during the first century was a corrosive and deadly fact that Christians were confronted with on every side. The religious rites in many of the Greek and Roman temples were sexually chaotic and exploitive; the cultural atmosphere in the whole of the Roman Empire was cruel. Seneca (4 B.C.–A.D. 65), a contemporary of Paul who acted as regent of the empire during the early years of Nero's reign as Caesar (54–68), was a careful chronicler of the decadence of Roman society. He wrote of his attendance at the games in Rome, "I came home more greedy, more cruel and inhuman, because I have been among human beings. By chance I attended a midday exhibition, expecting some fun, wit, and relaxation. . . . But it was quite to the contrary. . . . In the morning they throw men to the lions; at noon they throw them to the spectators. The crowd demands that the victor who has slain his opponent shall face the man who will slay him in turn" (Seneca, *Epist.* vii, xcv).

Marriage in Roman society survived as an institution only against great odds. Will Durant offers this assessment of the institution of marriage at the midpoint of the first century: "Marriage, which had once been a lifelong economic union, was now among many Romans a passing adventure of no great spiritual significance, a loose contract for the mutual provision of physiological conveniences or political aid" (vol. 3, p. 363).

The first-century Roman writer Juvenal noted that the wealthy wanted no children. "Poor women endure the perils of childbirth, and all the troubles of nursing . . . ; but how often does a gilded bed harbor a pregnant woman? So great is the skill, so powerful the drugs, of the abortionist . . . ; rejoice, give her the potion . . . for were she to bear the child you might find yourself the father of an Ethiopian" (Juvenal, vi, 592). Cynicism and luxury had combined to undermine marriage and the family.

Paul uses two words to describe the worth and importance of marriage: *holy* and *honorable*. Marriage has been drawn by God into his holy presence; he has granted it its worth and importance by his decision. The word *honorable* means literally "weighing heavily," and Paul uses this word to further impress upon his Christian friends the very great significance of this ancient relationship. Dietrich Bonhoeffer, in his letter to his sister on the occasion of her wedding, seeks to interpret the *holy* and *honorable* marriage theology of 1 Thessalonians 4 into a twentieth-century setting: "As God today adds his 'yes' to your 'yes' . . . by so doing he creates out of your love something quite new—the holy estate of matrimony. . . . In your love you see only the heaven of your own happiness, but in marriage you are placed at a post of responsibility. . . . It is God who gives it its special meaning and value, its own nature and privilege, its own destiny and dignity. . . . Thank him for it; thank him for leading you thus far. Ask him to establish your marriage, to confirm it, sanctify it, and preserve it. So your marriage will be 'for the praise of his glory.' Amen" (1953, p. 42).

Additional Notes

4:4 / His wife: The most thoughtful and complete examination of the New Testament understanding of marriage, in my view, is found in the book by Otto Piper, *The Christian Interpretation of Sex* (New York: Scribner, 1953). His discussion of 1 Thess. 4 is very useful. He sees the profound connection that exists between our relationships within marriage and our relationship with the world: "Since in the sex relationship we are dealing with a unity of the body, which remains indissoluble, sex life cannot be arbitrarily understood in a narrower sense. Our bodily character is the basis of all our life in this present world" (p. 126). See also the discussion of marriage in Helmut Thielicke, *The Ethics of Sex* (New York: Harper & Row, 1964). Thielicke notes the significant change in the understanding of the wife in marriage in the "order of redemption." "A final difference between the New Testament doctrine of Marriage and that of the Old Testament becomes evident in the way in which the status of the wife is changed. . . . In the table of household duties in Colossians 3:18–4:1, the subordination of the wife is assumed as before, and yet here it is given a new meaning in that both the wife and the husband are characterized by their being-in-the-Lord. So here the social hierarchy can no longer determine the nature of the wife" (p. 124).

4:3–7 / The relationship of the holiness of God and the holiness of the believer in regard to the human body and personal relationships is a theme that Paul will develop in more detail in his First Letter to the Corinthians (1 Cor. 6:12–20; see also 5:16–26).

Paul is clear in his insistence that the gift of holiness that the Christian receives from Jesus Christ through the Holy Spirit is not a static gift. It is a dynamic relationship between the believers and the source of holiness, Jesus Christ himself; it works its power out within our lives in terms of the way we relate to ourselves and to the people around us. This new source of meaning and life will often run crossgrain to the patterns of culture that surround our relationships. We should not be surprised by the conflict. "When faith really works, the will of God becomes our standard, no matter what the social patterns around us may be" (Hubbard, p. 934).

4:8 / Paul is fully aware of how severe the temptations against holiness really are for Christians in the Roman culture; therefore he reminds them of the support of God himself, who gives them his Holy Spirit.

7

First Things First

There is no need to write you about love for your fellow believers. You yourselves have been taught by God how you should love one another. ¹⁰And you have, in fact, behaved like this toward all the brothers in all of Macedonia. So we beg you, our brothers, to do even more. ¹¹Make it your aim to live a quiet life, to mind your own business, and to earn your own living, just as we told you before. ¹²In this way you will win the respect of those who are not believers, and you will not have to depend on anyone for what you need.

The Thessalonians are sincere Christians, yet something has diverted their discipleship. In the paragraphs that follow in Paul's two letters, it will become clear what has caused the entrapment of these young Christians.

Paul's approach to his friends has been a straightforward narration of his own relationship with them. He tells how they first believed; he reminds them of their beginnings and that their first convictions were not easy discoveries. They believed, and they suffered for their faith. They first became disciples of Jesus Christ against strong opposition. He expresses admiration for their present faith, hope, and love. He assures them of his own personal friendship.

Following this narrative section, Paul calls out to the Christians at Thessalonica practical and concrete marching orders from their Lord. The first ethical issue on which he focuses their attention is the most personal and private of the relationships, marriage (see Chapter 6). The second marching order has to do with the extended family.

4:9 / **There is no need to write you about love for your fellow believers.** The GNB has offered by the phrase **love for your fellow believers** an interpretive translation of the single Greek word *philadelphia*. *Philia* is the word for instinctive love, such as a person feels toward a family member. The word *adelphos* is the word for "brother." The GNB translation assumes that Paul has in mind the Christian extended family of believers rather than simply the biological inner family. The context that emerges in the sentences that immediately follow supports this interpretation. The only other place in Paul's writings that he makes use of the word *philadelphia* is in Romans 12:10, where the setting is almost identical to this passage. "Let love be genuine; hate what is evil, hold fast to what is good; love one another with *brotherly affection*; outdo one another in showing honor." Paul challenges the Thessalonians to love each other in the fellowship more and more. Something about their problems has created a preoccupation with other matters so that a slippage in this interpersonal working out of their faith, hope, and love has taken place. Paul warns them that love worked out toward their brothers and sisters in faith is not one option among other options but an essential part of their discipleship.

Another fascinating word choice by Paul is the term *theodidaktoi*. This compound word is made up of the word for God, *theos*, and the word for "teaching," *didache* (from which we get the English word *didactic*). This word appears only here in all of the New Testament, so that we are not able to trace other uses of it. Paul reminds his Christian friends that their mandate to love their Christian brothers and sisters is not of minor or secondary importance but is God taught, not simply taught in the doctrine of Paul or the church but actively **taught by God**.

4:11–12 / We have the beginning by Paul of a pastoral concern that will occupy much of the pastoral imperatives that follow in 1 and 2 Thessalonians. Something has happened at Thessalonica that has caused some of the Christians there to leave their jobs and become irresponsible in their behavior. We will consider the reasons for this and the underlying problems that caused this confusion as Paul's letter continues. At this point in the book we do not know the problems, but we have a clear picture of three practical, ethical concerns of the Apostle Paul for those first-century Christians. The disciple of Jesus Christ, who is called to holiness, who is drawn into the presence of God and stands beneath God's character in loyalty to his will has three clear mandates:

First, since marriage derives its meaning from God, Christians must relate within marriage in the light of God's will for marriage. Marriage is to be honored and held with profound respect because God has touched it and drawn it into his presence. This is not hard news to follow, but it is the profoundly good news that once again we discover how much we are worth when God touches our lives.

There is a second mandate or marching order. Because of the gospel of God we are to love one another more and more. The family of believers is more important than we realized before. The whole world is beloved in

Jesus Christ, so Paul has the "outsider" in his mind too (v. 12), but at this point he specifically challenges the Christians at Thessalonica to show love toward each other in the fellowship of believers.

The third mandate has to do with where the Christians work: **earn your own living**. The gospel affects that part of life too, and Paul does not leave it untouched by the implications of the reign of Jesus Christ. We are to work hard so that we win the respect of those who watch our lives.

Make it your aim: Paul has used a dynamic word in this sentence, *philotimeomai*, which means to "have as one's ambition," and that is the way the RSV translates this word in Romans 15:20, where Paul says, "Thus making it my *ambition* to preach the gospel." The only other place where the word appears in the New Testament is 2 Corinthians 5:9, "We make it our *aim* to please him." Paul urges the Thessalonians to strongly determine to live quiet and sober lives of hard work. In Paul's view, these young Christians need clear-cut objectives, so he uses this strong and ambitious word to communicate that concern.

The result of these clear-cut objectives will be that the non-Christian world will be drawn to consider the gospel that motivates such objectives. Paul is always missional, and even in such a context as this one, in which he is concerned for the fellowship of believers and the need for loving and hard-working Christians, he recognizes that the kind of lives that Christians lead will have an important effect upon the world that is watching. There is something refreshing about a person who has resources for feeling good about who he or she is, resources that are not derived from the usual assortment of cultural values and supports that everyone else in society depends upon. Here are people who do not cling to cultural symbols of power as the means of self-worth because there is another motivation for them to care, to love, and to be hard workers at their trade.

Paul's goal for the Christians at Thessalonica is that they first of all focus on and become clear about the motivational source of their life and that they follow this up with equal attention to the details of working it out where they meet people and where they work. His advice continues to ring true—the city is still looking on, waiting for people who are resolved at their center and practically effective at their edges.

Additional Note

William Neil has a brilliant discussion of this paragraph. "Paul's advice is eminently sane: work with your hands. That is their duty whether the end is approaching or not" (p. 87). "The Christian lives between the 'already' and the 'not yet.' He lives with the confidence that 'he who began a good work in you will carry it on to completion until the day of Jesus Christ' (Phil. 1:6)" (Richard Longenecker, in *Dreams, Visions and Oracles*, ed. Carl E. Armerding and W. Ward Gasque [Grand Rapids: Baker, 1977], p. 162). Paul counsels hard work and steady faithfulness for the time between "already" and "not yet."

8

Encourage One Another

Our brothers, we want you to know the truth about those who have died, so that you will not be sad, as are those who have no hope. [14]We believe that Jesus died and rose again, and so we believe that God will take back with Jesus those who have died believing in him.

[15]What we are teaching you now is the Lord's teaching: we who are alive on the day the Lord comes will not go ahead of those who have died.

[16]There will be the shout of command, the archangel's voice, the sound of God's trumpet, and the Lord himself will come down from heaven. Those who have died believing in Christ will rise to life first; [17]then we who are living at that time will be gathered up along with them in the clouds to meet the Lord in the air. And so we will always be with the Lord. [18]So then, encourage one another with these words.

What is the problem at Thessalonica? These new Christians who began their spiritual journey in truth and courage and love have now become entangled in theoretical worries about the future. The result of this entanglement has been harmful to their marriages, their interpersonal ethical relationships, and their work.

As we read closely the texts of 1 and 2 Thessalonians, we are able to trace at least three concerns that are troubling the believers at Thessalonica. First, some of the Christians are worried about the welfare of believers who have already died; they want to know what their status will be when Christ returns. The larger question is this: What is the hope of the Christian faith in the most practical terms? Is our hope only for the living? The text suggests that there were probably arguments and/or worries among the early Christians concerning this very practical question.

A second issue is that of the timing of the return of Jesus Christ. The first chapter of the Acts of the Apostles alerts all New Testament readers that from the very beginning of the life of the church, Christians look toward the return of Jesus Christ as the vindicated and reigning Lord: "This Jesus, who was taken up from you into heaven, will come in the same way as you saw him go into heaven" (Acts 1:11). In Thessalonica it has happened that some members within the church, or perhaps false prophets from outside the fellowship, have made their own chronological determination of the time of Christ's return, and these time predictions are the source of conflict and/or preoccupation within the fellowship.

The third problem is caused by the false teaching that Christ has already returned in some form and that this "second" coming is the secret knowledge of a group of specially chosen and spiritually equipped leaders.

What Paul must face is this: What are the Christians at Thessalonica to do with such specialized and esoteric questions as these?

The first question, about the state of believers who have already died, is very understandable. It is one indicator within the text that 1 Thessalonians is indeed very early in the body of New Testament books. If it is true that the early church expected the return of Christ to be soon, then this concern about the destiny and spiritual safety of those Christians who have already died is natural and inevitable.

The second problem is more complicated, since its implications for daily living are considerably more far-reaching. Those Christians who have timetables in their hands are hard to either comfort or exhort. For one thing, they feel a certain degree of spiritual pride at having decoded to their satisfaction the signs and mysteries of history to the point that they are able to make "second coming" predictions. Also, to their way of thinking, the more sincere a Christian is, the more willingly that Christian would be disposed to adopt the predicted timetable and then follow up that "assurance" by withdrawing from the ordinary patterns of daily life and work. Serious planning for the future responsibilities of life here and now might therefore be viewed as unspiritual and worldly.

The third problem at Thessalonica is neither a question of understandable worry about those who have already died nor one of the arrogance of timetables; this third issue is the result of false teaching that has its origin in a proto-Gnostic* outlook toward the Lord Jesus Christ and the promises of the Christian gospel.

The Christian gospel that broke in upon the first-century world with its affirmation and call to discipleship did not enter an empty arena. There were already present upon that stage a complex whirlwind of highly competitive ideas and ideologies. The gospel made sense to many of the

---

*"Gnosticism" is a term used by scholars to indicate a constellation of Oriental and Greek religious-philosophical ideas. Traditionally it was regarded as a Christian heresy, but most contemporary scholars consider it to be a broader phenomenon.

Jews, Romans, and Greeks who listened and watched as Christians like Paul, Peter, Apollos, Priscilla, and many other first-century believers shared their faith, their hope, and their lives. But within that arena, there were inevitably collisions of expectation and conviction. The New Testament portrays and carefully documents for its readers these collisions. Books like 1 and 2 Thessalonians help us to catch some of the ingredients of that coming together of the gospel and the whirlwind of first-century ideology. We sense the strain between the gospel and the synagogue. We also discover the collision course between the gospel of Jesus Christ and the intricate world of Greek ideas.

The mind-set in Greek thinking at the time of Paul's visits to the great cities of the Roman world was clearly defined in its rejection of the physical side of existence and its fascination with the spiritual side. There was a search underway for a grand entry into the spiritual realm of existence and a way of escape from the physical cycle of decadence and mediocrity. Many of those who were a part of this Greek mind-set when they first heard the gospel of Jesus Christ were fascinated by what they heard; but some of them quickly set about the task of domesticating the Christ of the gospel and redefining both his nature and his misison so that it would harmonize with their spiritual goals. This redefinition process, this entrapment of Jesus Christ, in its early stages is called by scholars proto-, or incipient, Gnosticism.

Early in the second century these groups formed themselves into the heretical Gnostic movements. They developed their own extensive literature and formed communities rivaling the early orthodox Christian church. Much of the writings of the early church fathers like Justin Martyr (ca. 100–ca. 165), Irenaeus (ca. 130–ca. 200), Hippolytus (ca. 160–ca. 236), and others are directed against the writings of these Gnostic groups. Through the writings of the church fathers, as well as the extensive discoveries of Gnostic writings themselves (for example, the Nag Hammadi manuscripts, uncovered by accident in Egypt in 1945 and 1946), modern scholars have been able to sort out the teaching and lifestyle of Gnosticism.

But the question remains: What hints do we have in 1 and 2 Thessalonians of proto-Gnostic dangers to the Christian believers? C. H. Dodd writes: "Gnosticism's authors are haunted by a sense of the misery and futility of human life in this world, and they connect this with our imprisonment in the material body, which is part of a material order of things. This material order is sharply contrasted with a higher order, entirely spiritual, having no contact with matter" (1960, p. 103).

One Gnostic writer, Marcus the Valentinian, explained the Gnostic hope of redemption in the following way. Redemption, according to Valentinian's teaching, comes from *gnōsis* (Greek for "knowledge"); "perfect redemption is simply knowledge of the unspeakable greatness; for defect and suffering or passion having come about through ignorance, the whole state of affairs produced by ignorance is dissolved by knowledge, so that knowledge is redemption of the inner man. It is not corporeal. . . . Redemption therefore must be spiritual. For the spiritual man is redeemed through knowledge" (quoted by Irenaeus *Adv. Haer.*, 1.14). This special knowledge (*gnōsis*) is the key to power and discovery of the secret, hidden code that sets the spiritual nature of a person free from the physical nature. Within Gnostic writings there is a strong antipathy toward the material world and anything that is physical. In the Gospel of Thomas, a document found among the Gnostic writings from Nag Hammadi, we find these words attributed to Jesus: "Woe to the flesh which hangs upon the soul! . . . Woe to the soul which hangs upon the flesh!" (Gospel of Thomas [110], 99:10–12). This same Gospel of Thomas tells of the mysterious presence of the Kingdom of God here in the world for those who have the knowledge to see its presence: "The kingdom of the father is spread out upon the earth, and men do not see it" (Gospel of Thomas [111], 99:12–27).

Basic to Gnostic thought is a rejection of physical reality and particularity in favor of spiritualization. One text from the Gospel of Thomas reveals how far this rejection of the physical had extended in Gnostic thought: "Simon Peter said to them: Let Marihass [Mary Magdalen] go away from us. For women are not worthy of life. Jesus said: Lo, I will draw her so that I will make her a man so that she too may become a living spirit which is like you men; for every woman who makes herself a man will enter into the kingdom of heaven" (Gospel of Thomas [112], 99:18–26).

What Paul therefore must cope with in his letters to the Christians at Thessalonica is, on the one hand, the hostility of certain members of the Jewish community who object to the Christian claims concerning Jesus Christ and, on the other hand, an incipient Gnosticism that rejects the body and yearns for spiritual breakthroughs. We see in the Thessalonian letters hints of that design of spiritualization in the false teaching that Jesus Christ had spiritually visited a favored few secretly and had granted to them special revelations and special secrets to enable them to escape from this physical world into the spiritual realm. Perhaps this is one reason these members of the church stopped working at their jobs.

Irenaeus warns the Christians of these teachers: "Certain men, rejecting the truth, are introducing among us false stories. . . . By their craft, by constructed rhetoric, they lead astray the minds of the inexperienced, and take them captive . . . for they upset many, leading them away by the pretense of knowledge from him who constituted and ordered the universe, as if they had something higher and greater to show them than the God who made the heaven and the earth and all that is in them" (Irenaeus, *Adv. Haer.* I, quoted in Richardson, p. 358). Perhaps the "higher" teachings had to do with the timetable of Christ's return or the teaching that he had already secretly returned.

If first-century Christians were to accept the proto-Gnostic outlook, we can see how the result in their lives would consist in a gradual evaporation of interest in the real world. Ethical concerns, family life, jobs, and earthly tasks would become less and less significant as the spiritual initiate began his or her journey toward spiritualization.

"The Gnostic cannot be affected by anything from the outside. Any kind of abstinence is out of the question, and indeed would be meaningless. There is no point in doing any work, no point in trying to make the world a better place, no point in training the soul for bliss. . . . Mankind is divided into two classes, the 'pneumatic' [spiritual] and the 'hylic' [earthly]. The fellowship realized among the pneumatics is based exclusively on a common detachment from the world" (Bultmann, 1956, p. 170).

Paul is well aware of the danger his beloved church at Thessalonica faces and that now manifests itself in their confusion about the true nature of their future hope. He will devote the remainder of these two letters to a clear and forthright discussion of these issues, grappling with the confusion at Thessalonica about the future and reminding the Thessalonians of the true doctrine concerning the future hope.

4:13 / Paul begins with the simplest of the problems. The word translated "died" is the Greek word *koimaō*, the ordinary Greek word for "sleep"; very early in classical Greek it is also used as a figure of speech for death. In the New Testament we have frequent use of this word as a synonym for death. One of the most interesting instances is in the Gospel of John (11:11), where our Lord says of Lazarus, "Our friend Lazarus has fallen asleep." The disciples misunderstand Jesus and think he meant that Lazarus was merely sleeping; he then tells them that he meant Lazarus had died. Paul uses *koimaō* as a word for death in several places, for example, 1 Corinthians 7:39, 15:18. So also does Peter in 2 Peter 3:4. (We derive the English words *coma, comatose,* from this word, as well as the word *cemetery.*)

4:14 / Paul writes in a very plain and direct fashion as he addresses the fears about the Christians who have already died. Jesus Christ has died and has conquered death; therefore, those who believe in him will share in his victory. This is the core of Paul's teaching, and its implications extend far beyond the particular question on the minds of the Thessalonians.

We who believe in Jesus Christ do not grieve as those who have **no hope** beyond this life. The question we must ask is, why is there this remarkable interruption of grief? It is not because Paul denies the existence of death. Death is real, and in this recognition Paul has a different hope from that of the Gnostics who, in the spiritualized hope of immortality, deny the reality of death. Paul's victory is grounded in the victory of Jesus Christ who has gone on ahead of us through death; therefore, when we face death, we face it with Jesus Christ alongside and ahead of us. Our hope is not that there is in us some indestructible spark of eternity that is absorbed into eternity. When we die, we die; but our hope is in Jesus Christ who has overcome death; because he lives we will live.

4:15-17 / Paul tells of the excitement and wonder that will be experienced with the return of Jesus Christ. We are told of the archangels' shout and of the sound of the trumpet. (Paul also mentions the trumpet in 1 Cor. 15:52.) It is clear that the return of Christ will be a dramatic event. Paul then assures his readers that those who are already dead are to share in this final victory in the same way as those who are alive at the time it happens. At this point, the apostle closes his teaching with a wonderful, uncomplicated sentence of assurance.

We will always be with the Lord: This is Paul's central and basic confidence. The Jesus Christ we have come to love and know at the center of our lives is the same Lord we will meet at history's end. The best hope is the simplest to understand. We will be with Christ and with each other too. There is a communion of saints that extends vertically down through history as well as horizontally within the time frame of our present existence.

4:18 / These are encouraging words for the Christians at Thessalonica as well as in our century. It is so precisely because they are so free from the entrapment of esoteric detail. Plain and direct, true and good: we will always be with the Lord. Can there be a better hope?

Paul's greatest affirmations come in the shortest sentences.

Additional Notes

Confusion about the future eschatological events has persisted through the centuries. Great upheavals were experienced in Europe at the approach of the year A.D. 1000; Moffatt tells of a citywide upheaval of expectation of the end of the world in Tripoli in 1899. Over against the panic that some experience because of predictions of the ending of history stands Paul's advice—**We will always be with the Lord, . . . encourage one another.**

4:15 / **The Lord's teaching**: Paul identifies his teaching in this letter with the teaching of Jesus Christ. The Thursday Evening Discourse of Jesus and the High Priestly Prayer of Jesus (John 13–17) give strong thematic endorsement from the gospel narratives to Paul's teaching in 1 Thessalonians.

4:18 / The word for encourage, *parakaleō*, means in its most basic sense "to come alongside." It is this word that will be pressed into service as the word for the Holy Spirit, the one who comes alongside (John 15:26).

9

Like a Thief

There is no need to write you, brothers, about the times and occasions when these things will	happen. ²For you yourselves know very well that the Day of the Lord will come as a thief comes at night.

5:1 / Paul makes use of two words for time that our text translates with the English words **times** and **occasions** ("seasons" in the RSV). The first word is *chronos*. This is a common word for time, especially in the sense of its duration. The English words *chronological* and *chronology* come from this Greek root and carry in English that same original intent. The second word used by Paul is *kairos*.

Kairos is an interesting word in classical Greek. "The linguistic development of the term clearly suggests that the basic sense is that of 'decisive or crucial place or point' whether spatially, materially or temporally" (*TDNT*, vol. 3, p. 455). The difference between the two words, therefore, is the difference between time as a decisive fixed moment and time as a measurable quantity of minutes, hours, and days. This same distinction holds for *kairos* and another New Testament word for time—the word *aiōn*, "era," "age," "eternity." Paul uses this term in 2 Thessalonians 1:9. "The characteristic thing about *kairos* is that it refers to a *point in time* defined by its content, while *aiōn* designates a duration of time, a limited or unlimited extent of time" (Cullmann, p. 39).

Kairos is an exciting and dramatic word. It should be noted, however, that New Testament writers make use of *chronos* in certain texts in a way that carries some of the same intensity and decisiveness we see in *kairos*. For example, in Galatians 4:4, Paul writes: "But when the fullness of the time came . . ." In this text we might expect Paul to use *kairos,* but he uses *chronos* in its place. The rule for interpretation in this case, as in all word studies, is to first carefully observe the use of the word in its sentence and the context of the passage under consideration. The warning by James Barr is important: "All lexical treatments which neglect the determinative importance of the syntactical context risk misrepresentation of the facts. . . . Only within their syntactical environment do words function" (p. 154).

The first principle of all Bible study is to closely observe the vocabulary choices of a writer at work within the text being studied and in other places where the writer employs the same term. Here in 1 Thessalonians 5:1 Paul has used *chronos* and *kairos* together; therefore, we are able with more confidence to discover his probable intention. This same choice of words also appears in Acts 1:7 in the statement of our Lord to his disciples in reply to their questions about the restoration of the kingdom to Israel: "It is not for you to know *chronos* or *kairos* [times or seasons] which the Father has fixed by his own authority." Both the timetables and the decisive moments of fulfillment belong to the Lord himself. Paul may have preached from this very story to the Christians at Thessalonica when he first shared the gospel with them; therefore, he reminds them of that early teaching by choosing the same words that he had used earlier.

Paul appears to scold the Thessalonians with regard to this matter: "You have no need to have anything written to you" (5:1, RSV). In other words, they ought to know enough already about this question; he feels that they had learned enough of the larger context to cover the details about which they are now spending so much time in controversy and preoccupation. A good teacher knows when students should be challenged to work out the implications of what they *already* know and apply those implications to the particular situation at hand. The Thessalonians already know about the authority and lordship of Jesus Christ; therefore, they are equipped to handle their own controversies about the timetables and the fulfillment events of history. Paul encourages his young friends in the faith to work through the implications of their central discovery concerning the reign of Jesus Christ, out at the edges where certain technical questions are certain to come to the surface.

5:2 / He makes an interesting use of the adverb *akribōs*, which means "accurately," "carefully." As a noun and verb, this word means "exact," "strict." The GNB translates this adverb **for you yourselves know *very well*.** Paul wants the Thessalonian Christians to do their own thinking, and he reminds them that their understanding of the great central truths has been accurate; their problem is that they have lost confidence in their own basic discovery. This has always been the problem of people who have been tempted by extremists or cultists who have specialized theories about small matters. The strategy of the cultist is to undermine the self-confidence of the Christian so that it becomes necesary to look to the cultist's theory for the correct and accurate latest truth. Paul grapples with this temptation in a very fresh and practical way. He refocuses attention back toward the true center. He reassures his readers that their faith in Christ is *accurate* and adequate, so that if they will now work through the implications of the Lordship of Christ—which they already know— their faith, their life together, and their work will make sense. What they must not do is to become snared in a fascination with secondary themes as if those themes were primary. The cultists have always had the advantage when it comes to secondary questions, because they have usually developed their most extensive doctrines at precisely the points where they can map, and thereby control, the more unfamiliar terrain. At the center, the ordinary Christian is well informed; but at the edges he or she may be less informed and therefore more easily exploited and deceived. Paul brings Christians back to the center and asks them to think for themselves about the meaning of the center for such edges as times and timetables.

The day of the Lord will come as a thief comes at night. Day of the Lord is a messianic phrase from the Old Testament (Amos 5:18; Isa. 2:12; Mal. 3:2, etc.). The phrase is also used frequently in the New Testament (Matt. 24:43; Luke 12:39; note also Rev. 3:3; 16:15; and 2 Pet. 3:10). The "day that belongs to the Lord" is the linguistic sense of this phrase, and we can rightly assume from the context in 1 Thessalonians that Paul has in mind the second coming of Jesus Christ when he uses this powerful phrase.

As a thief. In 2 Peter 3:10, there is almost the identical sentence: "But the Day of the Lord will come like a thief." In Matthew's Gospel, the same image is also used by our Lord (24:42–44). The key teaching in each place is that both the timetable and the meaningful moment belong to the Lord. Jesus makes this fact clear and nonnegotiable. "Therefore you must be ready, for the Son of Man is coming at an hour you do not expect" (Matt. 24:44). As his disciples we are to be ready; he is the one who decides everything else.

There is urgency in Paul's opening words in the fifth chapter. He realizes that if the Thessalonians become involved in elaborate methods and schemes designed to calculate the dates of the future fulfillment of history, they will have become preoccupied with the scheduling of a matter that is already safely in God's hands. Jesus had already warned his disciples against such a preoccupation, and now Paul joins in that warning.

The question we who read Paul's letter must ask today is this: Why is Paul so concerned about this matter? I believe the answer is to be found within the pastoral exhortations of 1 and 2 Thessalonians. Whenever there is a shift of focus away from the true center of faith, the results are destructive. For example, if a believer becomes confused about the source of salvation in the Lord Jesus Christ and his word and work, then the results are always damaging. Salvation is safely in Christ's hands, and when I forget that great central fact, it is then that legalism may replace faith so that I become my own savior.

It can happen in my relationship toward the world around me, too. We have all met people who have developed a "savior complex" toward people around them. In that case, they have forgotten the adequacy of Jesus Christ as the Savior, and often with the most sincere of motives, they then proceed to become redeemers. Such people are a danger not only to themselves but to the people around them. They seek to take on responsibility that was never intended for them. As disciples, they were meant to point to Christ, who is the true Redeemer, and to encourage their neighbors to discover salvation in Christ; instead, they try to become themselves the redeemer. With this, a disastrous shift has occurred. Jesus Christ is no longer the source of saving love and hope; instead, the well-meaning but confused disciples are trying to be and do what only the Lord of life can be and do. When we do this, we substitute ourselves and our good efforts for Jesus Christ as the heart of the gospel. We may honor him for his help, but in fact we make ourselves the good news; the result of this shift eventually is chaos. We and the movements we build are not able to bear such weight or such expectations. But had we stayed close to Jesus Christ, we would have known that he is the Savior and we are but witnesses in the world, to bring the world to Christ for healing. That healing occurs through the body of Christ, the church, for the benefit of those around our lives, but Christ himself is always the Savior Lord, and we are always mere Christians who have discovered his love and now want to share it.

This same sort of misfocusing has occurred at Thessalonica about the future return of Christ, with regard both to chronology and fulfillment. When Christians lose the sense of reverent restraint in such matters, a theory about the future replaces the Lord of the future at center stage. This has no good effects; those who buy into such teaching lose motivation concerning their present responsibilities. This shows up at Thessalonica as some become less interested in their marriages and drop out of their daily employment responsibilities. In some cases, there may even develop a gloomy panic or a hysterical euphoria, depending upon the particular emphasis of the favored teaching. Whatever the result, one thing is clear—such people leave their post of responsibility as disciples of Jesus Christ. They have instead become busybody "experts" in a subject matter that was never their mandate from the Lord. It is our responsibility to

Jesus Christ to stay faithfully at our post of mission and challenge here and now.

This problem at Thessalonica is still a problem today. I know of a respected evangelical pastor who has announced to his congregation that he fully expects the return of Jesus Christ during his own lifetime. This man, in his mid-fifties, has substituted a theory about history for the freedom of Jesus Christ to surprise us and establish his kingly reign in the way he chooses. Nothing positive and edifying for the members of this pastor's congregation will emerge from his chronological prediction. But what is most dangerous is that the people of God are encouraged to shift their attention away from the kingly reign of Christ toward the means and methods of this pastor's predictive analysis.

The Geman pastor Dietrich Bonhoeffer was confronted with the same kind of prophetic analysis during his imprisonment in the Germany of 1942. His remarkable essay *"After Ten Years,"* written to friends in December of that year, still stands as a clearheaded appeal to the Christian to keep the focus squarely upon Jesus Christ. He writes, "For most people, the compulsory abandonment of planning for the future means that they are forced back into living just for the moment, irresponsibly, frivolously, or resignedly; some few dream longingly of better times to come, and try to forget the present. We find both these courses equally impossible, and there remains for us only the very narrow way, often extremely difficult to find, of living every day as if it were our last, and yet living in faith and responsibility as though there were to be a great future: 'Houses and fields and vineyards shall again be bought in this land' (Jeremiah 32:15)" (1953, p. 15). We must always beware of those theories of the future that have the effect of demotivating our present responsibility. The gospel of Jesus Christ never has the effect of demotivating the present. The gospel motivates the present because its good center is the living Lord. He is the one who gives meaning to history's beginning, to its fulfillment, and to and within its present.

Additional Note

5:1 / **Times and occasions**: For additional discussion of the issues involved in the timing of biblical prophecy note the helpful discussions in *Dreams, Visions and Oracles,* ed. C. E. Armerding and W. W. Gasque (Grand Rapids: Baker, 1977). Note also the excellent discussion in G. W. Berkouwer, *The Return of Christ,* (Grand Rapids: Eerdmans, 1974).

The words of warning by Robert Clouse are helpful for this discussion: "Thus, prophetic teaching that is too detailed and leads to date-setting can harm the very cause of prophecy" (Armerding and Gasque, p. 36). Clouse also notes the danger of date-setting to the Christian's ethical mandate as well: "If Christ will surely return this year or next, it is easy for many to believe that attempts to alleviate social ills are useless" (p. 37). But the atmosphere in 1 and 2 Thessalonians is quite the opposite; it is the atmosphere of vigilance and daily obedience to the will of God in all of life.

10

To Belong to the Day

When people say, "Everything is quiet and safe," then suddenly destruction will hit them! It will come as suddenly as the pains that come upon a woman in labor, and people will not escape. ⁴But you, brothers, are not in the darkness, and the Day should not take you by surprise like a thief. ⁵All of you are people who belong to the light, who belong to the day. We do not belong to the night or to the darkness. ⁶So then, we should not be sleeping like the others; we should be awake and sober. ⁷It is at night when people sleep; it is at night when they get drunk. ⁸But we belong to the day, and we should be sober. We must wear faith and love as a breastplate, and our hope of salvation as a helmet. ⁹God did not choose us to suffer his anger, but to possess salvation through our Lord Jesus Christ, ¹⁰who died for us in order that we might live together with him, whether we are alive or dead when he comes. ¹¹And so encourage one another and help one another, just as you are now doing.

5:3 / The word translated **destruction** is a very strong and definite word. It means "ruin," "destruction." It is used only four times in the New Testament and each time by Paul (1 Cor. 5:5, 1 Tim. 6:9; and in two places in his letters to the Thessalonians, here, and 2 Thess. 1:9). In 2 Thessalonians 1:9, this powerful word will carry the meaning of separation from God. This separation crisis, Paul teaches us, will come suddenly. At this point the apostle surprises us with an illustration of suddenness that is not angry and despairing but alive with newness and hope, the example of childbirth. Paul tells his readers that the suddenness of the Day of the Lord's coming as judge will be just like labor pains connected with a child's birth—without warning. There will be no escape from this surprising interruption, the second coming of Jesus Christ, just as there is no escape from the event of birth when the time for birth has come.

5:4–5 / **You are people who belong to the light**: Paul now makes a statement that appears to counterbalance his opening statement in verse 2. Those who are disciples of the coming Lord should not be surprised by his coming. It is not that Paul has given the disciples an advantage as regarding the setting of dates or the establishment of timetables but that when Christ returns as reigning Lord we who know him will not be surprised, because the same Lord who stands at the beginning of history and at history's center is the Lord who meets us at the end of history. We know "the good thief" who comes; therefore, *he* is no surprise. The timing of the Lord of history is not ours to know, but the Lord of history we do know.

It is clear that Paul now makes a play on the word **day**. As all of history is bounded by the **Day of the Lord**, we who know Jesus Christ are already people of the "day." We live now in the present within the light of the Day of the Lord. The ultimate victory of Jesus Christ over darkness and death is what gives meaning to our present existence. We live here and now *from* that day and therefore *in* that day right now.

5:6–8 / Paul immediately spells out the implications of that fact. Since we as believers do not belong to the darkness, with its despair and separation from God, Paul calls his friends at Thessalonica to keep wide-awake and clearheaded. He speaks out against any dulling of the mind, whether by drugs (drunkenness) or by indolence (sleepiness). He calls for a wide-awake discipleship of men and women who live a fully active existence here and now, in and by the light of God.

How very far from all escapism is Paul! He calls out to Christians to stay in the real world, the twenty-four-hour cycle in which all other people live, and to stay with style. The mandate still rings true in the twentieth century. Our culture offers so many temptations toward the way of escapism and isolation. We are tempted to disconnect from society and human relationships, on the one side, to protect ourselves, and then to hurl ourselves into immediate and overwhelming personal relationships, on the other side, to satisfy ourselves. A gradual cynicism seeps into the process, and by inches the human story is caught up in a spiral toward despair. We may take pills to be dynamic, or at least to cope, and then pills to disconnect and go to sleep. Over against this temptation toward the dreamy world of constant and expensive tedium stands Saint Paul's demanding and vital portrayal of discipleship.

The moral and the intellectual implications are both evident in Paul's portrayal. Paul calls Christians to moral righteousness as a daily way of life. He also calls them to intellectual integrity as a people who are clearheaded and who want no part in soft thinking. The Christian does not approach God with the sleepy admiration of a mind drugged by religious subjectivism. God's good news is true and deserves to be thought about in broad daylight. The gospel thrives in such a setting, and it does not need any of the special nighttime supports of fatigue-induced compliance, or any other form of "heavenly deception."

5:8 / **Faith and love as a breastplate, and our hope of salvation as a helmet**. Now Paul informs his friends of the fact that the Lord himself equips his people for such a daytime mandate. Taking his image from the uniform of a Roman warrior, Paul suggests that faith, love, and hope are each so awesome when they find their source in Jesus Christ that they become strong armament to protect the Christian here and now.

5:9-10 / Whatever may happen to us, whether we live or die, we are safe in the salvation we have from Jesus Christ.

5:11 / **Encourage one another**: Paul's words are an encouragement to the Christians at Thessalonica. He has announced in clear terms that history is bounded by Jesus Christ, who indeed is the one who judges the earth and who comes again when we will not expect it. This boundary theme of Paul's will be expounded once again in his conclusion to chapter 8 of Romans (8:31–39). What is encouraging to us is that it is the same Jesus Christ who stands at history's summation. We live in this present age knowing of three sources for our worth: (1) the origins of the earth by God's decision; (2) the coming of Jesus Christ at history's center; and (3) the second coming of Jesus Christ at history's fulfillment.

At the center of this source for our meaning and hope is Jesus Christ, "who died for us in order that we might live." This is the radical interruption at the very center. The past and the future both point toward this center and authenticate its meaning for our lives. This is why Paul is encouraged. And this is why Paul's mandate to the Christians at Thessalonica is so "present tense" and contemporary in its implications. Because of Christ, who forms the boundary of history's future, the present is all the more important and exciting because we now know that so much more is at stake in what we do in our world than simply a few years of chronological existence. All that we do is to be judged and fulfilled by Jesus Christ. Both the judgment and the fulfillment are frightening and yet exciting facts to consider.

G. K. Chesterton wrote, "I have not minimized the scale of the miracle, as some of our milder theologians think it wise to do. Rather have I deliberately dwelt on that incredible interruption, as a blow that broke the very backbone of history. I have great sympathy with the monotheists, those of Islam and Judaism, to whom it seems a blasphemy, a blasphemy that might shake the world. But it did not shake the world; it steadied the world" (p. 274).

Just as a final score to the contest makes the sixty minutes and each play of a football game all the more exciting and meaningful, so the truth that Jesus Christ is the Lord of the ending as he is also Lord of the beginning and the center makes each separate part of the journey all the more significant.

Stay at Your Post

1 THESSALONIANS 5:12-28

We beg you, our brothers, to pay proper respect to those who work among you, who guide and instruct you in the Christian life. [13]Treat them with the greatest respect and love because of the work they do. Be at peace among yourselves.

[14]We urge you, our brothers, to warn the idle, encourage the timid, help the weak, be patient with everyone. [15]See that no one pays back wrong for wrong, but at all times make it your aim to do good to one another and to all people.

[16]Be joyful always, [17]pray at all times, [18]be thankful in all circumstances. This is what God wants from you in your life in union with Christ Jesus.

[19]Do not restrain the Holy Spirit; [20]do not despise inspired messages. [21]Put all things to the test: keep what is good [22]and avoid every kind of evil.

[23]May the God who gives us peace make you holy in every way and keep your whole being—spirit, soul, and body—free from every fault at the coming of our Lord Jesus Christ. [24]He who calls you will do it, because he is faithful.

[25]Pray also for us, brothers.

[26]Greet all the believers with a brotherly kiss.

[27]I urge you by the authority of the Lord to read this letter to all the believers.

[28]The grace of our Lord Jesus Christ be with you.

5:12-13 / Chapter 5 seems to support the possibility that there are stresses that have developed within the church at Thessalonica due to a rift between the leaders in the church and the people at large. Three key words dominate Paul's counsel: **respect**, **love**, and **peace**.

Paul makes use of the Greek word *oida*, which is usually translated "to know" but in this context carries the intent of "to know the worth of." Moulton and Milligan's lexicon points out the fact that this word is used commonly to mean "know in contexts which suggest full, accurate knowledge" (MM, p. 439). They go on to indicate that the word may also carry the meaning "appreciate," "respect" and cite examples of this in classical Greek usage. Paul now makes this special and subtle use of *oida*; he asks these young Christians to recognize the worth of their leaders. It is thoughtful respect that Paul is advocating, a respect that requires thought as well as submission of the will. Paul wants his friends to think through their relationships and to honor each other. It is a form of regard that is considered and understood. It is the kind of respectfulness that is advocated for people who have been set free from the obedience of tyranny; it is respect that I have decided upon myself, not that which is forced upon me. Paul is not interested in the respect of terror, like that toward the Roman emperor, but the respect that grows out of relationship and community.

Another fascinating word choice appears in this paragraph. Paul makes use of a triple intensive adverb (*hyper-ex-perissou*), which is then attached to the verb "to think," "consider" (*ēgeomai*). George Milligan translates this sentence as follows: "Hold them in love exceedingly highly" (p. 72). This superlative way of expression shows how deeply Paul cares about these relationships that the Thessalonian Christians have toward each other. They need to express more love toward each other, and with enthusiasm. Finally, Paul encourages them to be at peace. What has probably happened is that the controversies concerning future events have strained the relationships within the fellowship. They not only need to value the solid leadership and integrity of their regular leaders, but they also need to calm down and slow down. Every church will thrive by following that counsel: respect, enthusiastic love, and healthy peaceableness in interpersonal relationships.

5:14 / **Warn the idle**: The word that Paul makes use of here is *ataktos*, a fascinating choice. What is especially interesting is that Paul uses it as a noun, verb, and adverb some four times within 1 and 2 Thessalonians, yet the word appears nowhere else in the New Testament. The prefix *a* in Greek connotes the negative "no," as, for example, in the word *agnostic* where it means "no knowledge." The word *taktos* means "fixed" or "appointed," as in its use in Acts 12:21. Therefore, this word *ataktos* means "away from your post" or "not at your post." It is a military word, used of a soldier who is *un*disciplined or *dis*orderly. The sense of the word is not simply that a person is carefree and unoccupied, but that the person is derelict in his or her duty. In classical Greek it often means riot and rebellion (MM, p. 89). Paul's concern is that the Christians at Thessalonica stay at their post of responsibility and not fade away because of their preoccupation with other matters.

Encourage the timid: The word for timid here is a word that could be translated "worried" or "discouraged." One of the results of pressure and intensity of opposition is that people become obsessive and fearful. Added together, these are the chief causes of people being lured from their posts of responsibility. Paul now urges the Christian fellowship to face up to the debilitating pressure that produces such fearfulness. He wants the Christians to encourage each other, especially those whose "spirit is all but broken and who are on the verge of giving up" (Ward, p. 115).

Paul is never a sentimentalist, and in this advice his optimism and encouragement is not the glad-handed "cheering up" of shallow encouragement but, rather, confidence grounded in the faulthfulness of God, "for this is the will of God."

Help the weak: Another mark of a time of intensity and pressure is that people wear out from fatigue. Paul is as aware of "burnout" in his century as we are in our century; exhaustion is not a sin, but it never feels very good. Paul does not give detailed advice; instead he challenges the Christian fellowship to **help** the weak. He leaves the details to the helpers. What is obvious is that the person who is tired out needs another shoulder alongside.

Be patient with everyone. Here Paul chooses the verb *makrothu-meō*, which means "to have patience" in the sense of longstanding endurance and steadfastness. *Thumos* is the word for "intense desire" in the New Testament; hence "wrath," as in Ephesians 4:31, "Let all bitterness and *wrath* and anger . . . be put away." *Makrothumeō* is made up of *thumos* plus the prefix *makro*, which means "far away from." The quality of patience that is implied is tough and durable in the face of intense pressure. It is the patience that puts up with hardships and has the ability to endure. It is the decision to stay away from fury and wrath. Paul is calling for the kind of quiet strength that is willing to hang on to the faith and to the people of the faith through dangers and intense pressures. This is the patience that resists the temptation toward fury or toward the rage of disappointment. What good to the world and to God's Kingdom are we as Christians if we write each other off and easily become bitter toward one another? What we need is *makrothumos*, the kind of patience that resists the way of anger and instead takes the more challenging way of identification and ministry.

5:15 / **See that no one pays back wrong for wrong**. There are themes in 1 and 2 Thessalonians that the Apostle Paul will greatly enlarge and extend in his later books. Such is the case with the brief sentence we now observe. In Romans 12:14–21, Paul expands upon this brief, one-line statement and develops the theological underpinning for his exhortation. Here Paul is introducing a new way of responding to an ancient crisis. He argues that the task of the Christian is to introduce a new ingredient into the real experience of wrong. We are not to respond to wrong with more wrong but dare to introduce a new and more creative element. **Make it your aim to do good to one another and to all people.** We are to have a positive, creative policy in interpersonal relationships and not an unimaginative, negative reflex-policy. In the latter case we are simply reactors to the acts of others; in the former, we share in the creation of a new good. We do not ourselves create the new good; it comes to us from God. But as we share its health and healing power in the world, it is indeed new as far as the world is concerned.

5:16–18 / Be joyful always. "Joy" (*chara*) is the root word for grace (*charis*) and also for thanksgiving (*eucharistia*). Paul now encourages his friends to sing out in joy and thanksgiving because of the grace of the Lord Jesus Christ. All three words are placed together by Paul in these final words of encouragement in the letter. God wants us to enjoy his love. The world situation is not the determining factor; rather it is our sudden perception of God's goodness that causes joy; the situation does not make the real difference, because the source of thanksgiving is not only our journey but also the companion of our journey. This awareness by Paul of the source of joy is the secret to his doctrine of thanksgiving. C. S. Lewis has captured the sense of this radical joy in his novel *The Horse and His Boy*. When the human hero of the story, Shasta, makes the discovery that the large presence beside him on the perilous mountain trail is the great lion Aslan, some remarkable things happen inside of Shasta. " 'Who are you?' asked Shasta. 'Myself,' said the voice, very deep and low so that the earth shook; and again 'Myself,' loud and clear and gay; and then the third time 'Myself,' whispered so softly you could hardly hear it, and yet it seemed to come from all round you as if the leaves rustled with it.

"Shasta was no longer afraid that the voice belonged to something that would eat him, nor that it was the voice of a ghost. But a new and different sort of trembling came over him. Yet he felt glad too" (New York: Collier, 1970), p. 159. Lewis is describing the joy of the recognition of God's living presence and, what is most important for us, the love and faithfulness of that unseen Companion.

5:19–22 / Do not restrain the Holy Spirit. The verb is literally "quench" or "extinguish," as in Mark 9:44, 46, 48. Paul does not want the Christians to attempt to suppress what God is doing in their midst. Therefore, he urges them to welcome prophetic affirmation in the church. But he follows this encouragement with the serious task of evaluation. He challenges them to **put all things to the test**. *Dokimazō* ("to test" or "examine") makes it clear that we are to think through carefully the affirmations and claims being brought forward in the church. Paul will later use this word in his Letter to the Romans, where it is part of a promise he makes to the Romans that as they present themselves to Christ and then challenge the false value systems of this age they will "*prove* what is the will of God; that it is good, acceptable, perfect" (Rom. 12:2). His point in Romans 12 is that the Roman Christians will test it out for themselves and discover how true and good and complete is God's will for life. To the Thessalonian Christians, he recommends an open style of life toward one another rather than suspicion and fear of one another. Fear and suspicion produce an atmosphere that is damp and oppressive, which quenches the fire of God's ministry in their fellowship. Paul also matches that openness with the encouragement to test and verify, as the scientist does with each hypothesis, in order to discern the goodness of the affirmations that are being presented in the church. The word for **good** is *kalos*, which carries the connotation of "excellent" or "accurate," therefore "faithful." The criteria for this testing is the Lord Jesus Christ, from whose coming every Christian lives now in the present. Jesus Christ who stands at history's beginning, at its center, and at its close is the criterion by which the messages of the prophets in the church are tested.

The same criterion stands firm today as the sole criterion for the testing of doctrine: Jesus Christ the living Center and the witness that surrounds him, the Old Testament in anticipation and the New Testament in verification. The biblical authority derives its authority in borrowed fashion from this living Center, Jesus Christ. The questions we must ask are: Does the teaching affirm our union with Jesus Christ and encourage that union? Does the doctrine submit to the lordship of Jesus Christ?

5:23–24 / Paul does not want the Christians to be so worried about each other and the issue of doctrinal accuracy that they quench what God is doing by his Holy Spirit to assure the believers in their union with Christ. On the other hand, Paul wants the Christians to care deeply about the faithfulness of all teaching to the true center of our hope, Jesus Christ the Lord. He wants warm and open, and, at the same time, wise and clear-thinking, Christians at Thessalonica. This sort of people is needed in every city of every age.

Keep your whole being—spirit, soul, and body: The New Testament has a holistic understanding of human personality. It is the total self that is beloved by God; therefore, for Paul there can be no spiritualism or spiritual escapism for the Christian. The mystery of the Christian hope is that the whole person is beloved, is set free in redemption, and will be fulfilled in resurrection.

Another remarkable word choice by Paul makes this total view of personality vivid for his readers. The Greek word *holoteleis* is made up of *holos* ("whole," "entire," "complete") and *telos* ("end," "fulfillment"). Therefore, the word is best translated "quite complete." This word appears only here in the New Testament. Once again we have an example of Paul's skillful use of the Greek language to communicate powerfully and accurately. Make no mistake about it, Paul wants no nonsense about spiritual escapism in the church.

5:26 / **Greet all the believers with a brotherly kiss**. The tradition of the kiss as a sign of warm affection was widespread throughout the Mediterranean world of the first century. This becomes one more sign of the affectionate relationship between Paul and this young church in Thessalonica. The fellowship of believers was more than an intellectual or moral or spiritual comradeship; they were family, and they really cared for each other. They wanted to hug each other.

5:27 / Paul then instructs those who receive his letter to share its message with the whole church. There are, I think, two concerns that stand behind Paul's instruction. First, Paul does not want factionalism to emerge in the church; he therefore will not permit any small group within the fellowship to claim his letter as especially for them. Paul's second concern is more obvious. He feels that what he has written is of such importance that he wants the whole community to hear it.

He closes his letter with a final wish that the surprise love gift that comes from the Lord Jesus Christ will be with the Christians in Macedonia. What an exciting and powerful faith we have! We are not only able to send letters to each other but we are able to share in the alive love of Jesus Christ though we are miles apart. All of this is because Jesus Christ lives and he cares for the ordinary Christians at Thessalonica just as much as he cares for their friend Paul at Corinth.

Additional Notes

5:14 / See the long article on the word *makrothumeō* ("patience") in *TDNT*, pp. 374–87. "It is not just that all members of the Community stand in need of forbearance and patience, for what is based on human need is no virtue . . . it is the fruit of the Spirit" (p. 383).

5:15 / **Do good**. "While First Thessalonians unfolds many great doctrinal revelations, it closes with a very practical note (John T. Walvoord, *The Thessalonian Epistles* [Grand Rapids: Zondervan, 1976], p. 56). This practical emphasis becomes a vital part of the means that the Christian church has of testing the teaching and program content of its own life.

12

Worthy of His Kingdom

2 THESSALONIANS 1:1-5

From Paul, Silas, and Timothy—
    To the people of the church in Thessalonica, who belong to God our Father and the Lord Jesus Christ:
    ²May God our Father and the Lord Jesus Christ give you grace and peace.
    ³Our brothers, we must thank God at all times for you. It is right for us to do so, because your faith is growing so much and the love each of you has for the others is becoming greater. ⁴That is why we ourselves boast about you in the churches of God. We boast about the way you continue to endure and believe through all the persecutions and sufferings you are experiencing. ⁵All of this proves that God's judgment is just and as a result you will become worthy of his Kingdom, for which you are suffering.

The second letter of Paul to his friends at Thessalonica was written very soon after the first. Paul has heard further reports of the situation in the church; he now has available to him more details about the false teaching the church is confronting, including the news that these false prophets have purported to have a letter from Paul himself, which they claim gives support to their special theories (2 Thess. 2:2). Therefore, Paul quickly responds with this second letter. Second Thessalonians repeats themes that have been stated in the first letter, but it expands upon the doctrinal question that continues to trouble the church, namely, the teaching concerning the second coming of Jesus Christ.

1:1-2 / The opening greeting follows the same formal style that Paul made use of in 1 Thessalonians. We now have set in place a way of writing that shall be the literary mark of the apostle in all future letters as well. These greetings, together with concluding remarks (2 Thess. 3:16–18), will form an autograph of the apostle. In every letter Paul will greet his readers with the words, **grace** and **peace** from God the Father and the Lord Jesus Christ. These words are a prayer in favor of his readers as Paul claims the surprise gift of love and the peace that comes from God and his Son toward us as we read his letter.

1:3 / **Because your faith is growing . . . and the love each of you has . . . is becoming greater**: Paul honors the Thessalonian Christians once again for their faith and their love. For Paul **love** and **faith** are both dynamic, growing experiences of discipleship. These words do not describe a static or nodding assent; instead, they describe an increasing, widening possibility of grace at work in the lives of those who trust God. Love is what happens not only *within* our lives as believers but also *through* our lives toward the world around us. Paul is describing the source of Christian ethics; his ethic is an ethic that moves out from fullness toward need. It is not an ethic of fear or guilt in which a believer is commanded to love; rather, we are first to experience the love and the faithfulness of God, and from that profound source, it is possible to reach out in love to the world. The command grows out of the prior fact of God's grace toward us.

The assurance of the steadfastness and trustworthiness of God, which is discovered and verified en route as the Christian disciple lives the life of faith, becomes the foundation upon which it is possible to build creative and loving interpersonal relationships. It is never a simple matter to love one's neighbor, or even one's brother and sister. There are stresses and temptations; there are a hundred things that argue against the ethic of love with its obligations. Self-interest, fear, doubt, anger—each of these works against ethical responsibility. Therefore, Christians must have the kind of faith and love that is durable in the face of stress.

"There are two essential characteristics of Christian ethics," writes Otto Piper. "First, all aspects of Christian life are ultimately rooted in God's purpose of redemption. . . . Second, the life of faith has a subject matter of its own, that is, how to believe in God while living in a world that is not divine" (p. 2). The first characteristic is the source of Christian life and discipleship, and the second has to do with the setting in which we must live out the love and assurance we have experienced. Paul now turns his attention to that second characteristic.

1:4 / **You continue to endure and believe through all the persecutions and sufferings**: We who are Christians must live as disciples in a less than ideal setting. It is within the ordinary twenty-four-hour cycle of daily existence that discipleship is lived and must survive. Paul makes use of the present tense of the verb **endure**; the apostle honors the Thessalonians because they are enduring here and now, in spite of the stresses they encounter. The capital cities within the Roman Empire were the hardest places for Christians to survive, because of the fanatical intensity of emperor worship in those centers. Also, as we have already observed, the young church at Thessalonica was under considerable pressure from the members of the synagogue who were opposed to the growing Christian fellowship.

1:5 / Paul goes on to make one more very significant observation: **This proves that God's judgment is just**. What does the apostle mean by this? I think Leon Morris is correct in connecting this sentence to the total context of the preceding sentences (1956, p. 115). Paul's point is that God's justice and decision is now validated in what has happened in the lives of the Christians, that is, in their endurance, faith, and courage in the face of great hardship.

Paul goes on to say that these believers have been counted **worthy of** [God's] **Kingdom** because of the grace of God at work in their lives and their faithful courage under intense pressure. Behind the Apostle Paul's words, we can hear the words of Jesus, "Well done, good and faithful servant" (Matt. 25:21, 23). Paul has described "the weight of glory." This amazing promise is true; "it is almost incredible, and only possible by the work of Christ, that some of us, that any of us who really choose, shall actually survive the examination, shall find approval, shall please God. To please God is to be a real ingredient in the divine happiness, . . . to be loved by God, not merely pitied, but delighted in as an artist delights in his work or a father in a son—it seems impossible, a weight or burden of glory which our thoughts can hardly sustain. But so it is" (Lewis, 1949, p. 10).

Additional Note

Kingdom language is common in the Old and New Testaments. The word was used by Paul in 1 Thess. 2:12, and in that setting it is seen as the possession of God, "his own Kingdom." Kingdom in Paul is not seen in territorial terms but rather in relationship terms. The Kingdom is the kingly reign of Christ to which we believers belong as we trust in Christ's reign. Best emphasizes the future significance of Kingdom and interprets this text totally in that sense: "the eschatological community of the redeemed at the parousia" (p. 255). He therefore interprets this passage as a future promise by Paul to the Christians at Thessalonica. Neil, in my view, is more accurate about Paul's full intention in his insistence that Paul intends not only a future hope by the use of the word Kingdom but also a present hope and experience as well. "Paul wants to comfort them both with reference to the present and the future." (p. 143). This means that the future promise of Kingdom is experienced by the suffering believers here and now in that the King of the Kingdom is with us. It is important to keep the present and future united in order to make sense of New Testament Kingdom theology.

13

A Day of Judgment

2 THESSALONIANS 1:6–12

God will do what is right: he will bring suffering on those who make you suffer, [7]and he will give relief to you who suffer and to us as well. He will do this when the Lord Jesus appears from heaven with his mighty angels, [8]with a flaming fire, to punish those who reject God and who do not obey the Good News about our Lord Jesus. [9]They will suffer the punishment of eternal destruction, separated from the presence of the Lord and from his glorious might, [10]when he comes on that Day to receive glory from all his people and honor from all who believe. You too will be among them, because you have believed the message that we told you.

[11]That is why we always pray for you. We ask our God to make you worthy of the life he has called you to live. May he fulfill by his power all your desire for goodness and complete your work of faith. [12]In this way the name of our Lord Jesus will receive glory from you, and you from him, by the grace of our God and of the Lord[a] Jesus Christ.

a. our God and of the Lord; *or* our God and Lord.

1:6 / **God will do what is right**. The word *dikaios* ("just" or "right") is a word of major significance in Paul's vocabulary. It is the word that describes the character of God. God is just, and because of the justice that exists in the very character of God himself, justice is built in to the created order. In this passage Paul portrays both the salty and the joyous sides of that justice. There is vengeance in the judgment of God, and there is also healing; they stand together. Karl Barth has caught this twofold sense of God's judgment in his commentary on the sentence in the Apostle's Creed that describes the coming of Jesus Christ, who "comes to judge the quick [living] and the dead." "In the biblical world of thought," he writes, "the judge is not primarily the one who rewards some and punishes the others; he is the man who creates order and restores what has been destroyed. We may go to meet this judge, this restoration or, better, the revelation of this restoration, with unconditioned confidence, because He is the judge" (p. 135). Barth goes on to warn against those theological interpretations that eliminate the negative sense of holy judgment. "To the seriousness of the thought of judgment no injury will be done, for there it will be manifest that God's grace and God's right are the measure by which the whole of humanity and each man will be measured. . . . That there is such a divine NO is indeed included in this *judicare*. . . . There is a decision and a division, but by him who has interceded for us."

1:7-8 / The point is made clear by Paul in his letter. The one who is the final judge is Jesus Christ the Redeemer. He is the one who finally weighs and measures our lives and therefore only he has the right to say the last word about any human being. There is good news, therefore, even in the affirmation about judgment. It is a good judge that we meet in history's end, but judge he is and judge he will.

Notice that the result of the coming of this judge is twofold: (1) the broken ones who now suffer under the terror of unrighteousness and yet endure in their trust in God's character will be healed (v. 7); (2) those who have decided against God's character will receive as their judgment the awful agreement of God with their decision (v. 8).

1:9-10 / This means that the punishment of final judgment, according to Paul, is separation **from the presence of the Lord.** The choice that such a human being has made against God's love and reign is then sealed and extended into eternity (v. 10). We now have Paul's definition of hell. Hell, according to Saint Paul, would be a human being at an infinite distance from God. It is the ultimate silence of God. Notice that in this passage the freedom of the human being is preserved even to the extent that such a tragic and bad choice could take place. It is a sign of the respect that God has for human beings that our integrity is preserved, even at the edge of such an awesome and ultimate chasm. In verse 7 ("when the Lord Jesus appears"), Paul makes use of the Greek word *apokalypsis*, which means "surprising breakthrough" or "uncovering." This word now joins with the other word *parousia*, translated in 1 and 2 Thessalonians by the English word "coming." "At his coming, his grand appearance" is the sense of the word *parousia*. "His surprising unveiling" is the sense of *apokalypsis*. Paul reminds the Thessalonians of the fact of the surprising manifestation of Jesus Christ that awaits human history, therefore, he prays that we as God's people will be a good people, fully at work and growing in our faith so that we are ready for the fulfillment of history at every moment, prepared for any surprise and therefore prepared for the greatest surprise of all.

Paul makes a remarkable connection in verse 10 between the glory of Jesus Christ and the glory of his disciples. In some mysterious sense, we who believe in Christ will share in his glorification. Paul puts it this way:

Christ will be glorified in his people. See also Romans 8:28, where Paul makes this same point.

He continues his line of reasoning to its logical conclusion in verses 11 and 12. He prays that the glory of the name of Christ might be seen in us.

A passage like this one takes us so by surprise that we have a hard time really hearing what it says. We have been so accustomed to contemplating the sinfulness of Christians, our hypocrisy and failing, that Paul's words here in 2 Thessalonians 1 are unreal for us. How well we know that we and our churches are a scandal to the reputation of God on the earth (Dorothy Sayers has powerfully sketched in that fact of scandal. She describes the church as the Third Humiliation of God). But now Paul surprises us: God is proud of us, we are his joy; and he will startle the whole of creation, both heaven and earth, with what happens in our lives by his grace. We have here in 2 Thessalonians the first glimpses of this theme that Paul will expand further in Romans 8:18–25 and Ephesians 1:11–23.

Additional Note

Ernest Best has an excellent discussion of the significance of "name" as it appears in this text (p. 271). See also the word study in *TDNT* (pp. 242–82). We must realize the significance of names and naming in the biblical world of thought in order to catch the full significance of Paul's decisive use of **name** in this text (v. 12). Name reveals both identity and authority. A name "is the power which is very closely associated with the bearer and which discloses his nature" (*TDNT*, p. 243).

14

Lawlessness and Restraint and Victory

Concerning the coming of our Lord Jesus Christ and our being gathered together to be with him: I beg you, my brothers, ²not to be so easily confused in your thinking or upset by the claim that the Day of the Lord has come. Perhaps it is thought that we said this while prophesying or preaching, or that we wrote it in a letter. ³Do not let anyone deceive you in any way. For the Day will not come until the final Rebellion takes place and the Wicked One appears, who is destined to hell. ⁴He will oppose every so-called god or object of worship and will put himself above them all. He will even go in and sit down in God's Temple and claim to be God. ⁵Don't you remember? I told you all this while I was with you. ⁶Yet there is something that keeps this from happening now, and you know what it is. At the proper time, then,

the Wicked One will appear. ⁷The Mysterious Wickedness is already at work, but what is going to happen will not happen until the one who holds it back is taken out of the way. ⁸Then the Wicked One will be revealed, but when the Lord Jesus comes, he will kill him with the breath from his mouth and destroy him with his dazzling presence. ⁹The Wicked One will come with the power of Satan and perform all kinds of false miracles and wonders, ¹⁰and use every kind of wicked deceit on those who will perish. They will perish because they did not welcome and love the truth so as to be saved. ¹¹And so God sends the power of error to work in them so that they believe what is false. ¹²The result is that all who have not believed the truth, but have taken pleasure in sin, will be condemned.

2:3 / **Do not let anyone deceive you in any way**: The Thessalonian Christians have been confronted by false teaching, so Paul now challenges both the false doctrine and the unsettled atmosphere in the church that enabled the false teaching to make headway in the first place. The young church has become confused about doctrine concerning the second coming of Jesus Christ (see earlier discussion). Has Christ already returned? Paul's name and a supposed letter from him have evidently played a part in the special doctrines that were advocated to these Christians (v. 2). The apostle denies any such letter or teaching and then proceeds to offer some clarifying statements on this question for his readers.

For the Day will not come until the final Rebellion takes place. Verses 3–12 form the most difficult sentences in the whole of the two letters to interpret with certitude. The vocabulary is very vigorous, and though some parts of the argument are difficult to interpret, nevertheless the total force and intent of the passage is clear.

Paul first reminds the Thessalonians that the Day of the Lord will not come until the runaway rebellion takes place. The word translated **Rebellion** is *apostasia*. It means "abandonment" and is used in this particular form only one other time in the New Testament (Acts 21:21). From this root another form (*apostasion*) is used as a word for divorce (Matt. 19:7 and Mark 10:4).

In connection with this abandonment, there is to appear **The Wicked One . . . who is destined to hell** (cf. vv. 6, 8, and 9). This is a curious translation by the GNB. The RSV offers a more exact translation of the precise language of Paul: "The man of lawlessness, the son of ruin." This foe will be revealed in a surprising way. The verb *apokalypsis* is again used here, the same word used of the revelation of the Lord Jesus in 1:7. This man of lawlessness makes claims as to his own deity: literally, "showing himself that he is God" (RSV).

2:5 / Paul continues his reminder to the Thessalonians. All of this teaching should not be new to them. They should already know of these facts from Paul's teaching when he was with them as the founder of their church.

2:6 / **Yet there is something that keeps this from happening**. The verb *katechō* is used by Paul in both this verse and verse 7. It is translated "restrain" in the RSV. It means literally "to hold back." These sentences are very difficult to interpret. What is it that restrains or holds back the runaway abandonment of the lawless one? Paul reminds the Thessalonians that they know the identity of this restraining force: **You know what it is**.

There have been many different interpretations. Some have argued that the church itself is the restraining force, or the Holy Spirit at work in the church. This view is offered in the *Scofield Reference Bible*: "This person can be no other than the Holy Spirit in the church" (p. 1272). But the problem with this view appears in the next verse, where the restraining force is spoken of as **taken out of the way**.

Leon Morris argues that "it is better to see in the restraining power a reference to the principle of law and government" (p. 129). F. F. Bruce agrees: "My own view is that Paul was referring to the forces of law and order which acted as a restrain on the forces of lawlessness for the time being; when the forces of law and order were removed, then the forces of lawlessness would break forth" (1973, p. 112). This law-and-order view is very ancient and was proposed also by the church fathers Tertullian (ca. 160–ca. 220) and Chrysostom (ca. 347–ca. 407). Paul's reference to the authority of the state as a "terror to evil" in Romans 13:1, 3 also gives support to this view.

John Calvin held yet another view. He saw the gospel and its spread around the world as the restrainer. "I seem at least to hear Paul discoursing as to the universal call of the Gentiles—that the grace of God must be offered to all. . . . This therefore, was the delay, until the career of the gospel should be completed" (p. 333).

2:8-10 / **The Wicked One will come with the power of Satan**. Once again the exact term is not **wicked** but "lawless one." The word **Satan** that appears in this text is one of the terms used in the New Testament to describe the devil. The word literally means "adversary." This Semitic word transliterated into Greek is used synonymously with the terms *diabolos* ("slanderer") and also the term *ho poneros* ("the evil one") and *apollyōn* ("destroyer"). This last term is used only in Revelation 9:11. According to the passage, the lawless one is under the authority of Satan or is Satan himself. The New Testament writers all take with complete seriousness the existence of Satan and his power. That power is seen in this passage as very great but by no means total or final. The outer boundary of the authority of Jesus Christ is greater still. Paul's teaching concludes with the affirmation that the Lord Jesus Christ will destroy Satan. Within the context of this passage, Satan exists as personal opposition against the character and person of God at the higher, cosmic realm of the created order. Satan stands over against humanity as well; he is the deceiver and tempter of humanity.

2:11-12 / Paul concludes this paragraph with a difficult and complex observation: **And so God sends the power of error**. The very possibility of Satan is only a reality because God has allowed a freedom at the cosmic level of creation such as the freedom he provides by his sovereign decision at the human level of creation. Leon Morris points out that in the biblical world of thought "the powers of evil are allowed no independent existence. . . . In particular God uses the evil consequences of sin as part of the punishment of the sinner (Morris, p. 134).

It is important to note that the downward spiral of the delusion is an event that follows the bad choice made by those persons who in the use of their freedom "did not welcome and love the truth so as to be saved" (Calvin, 1953, vol. 3, p. 229). Therefore, it is clear that the freedom of human beings is preserved in Paul's portrayal. What happens is that "by a bad use of freedom man loses both himself and his freedom" (ibid.).

We must make some final observations about this passage. "Lean is better than luxurious" is the important rule for all interpretation of Scripture, and it is a vitally important rule for our interpretation of these sentences. From our place in time, we are not aware of certain particular interpretive clues that the Thessalonians already knew about from Paul's instruction when he had been with them earlier. Therefore, we must be satisfied to confine our interpretive explanations to the matters that become clearest from the text. What is clearest is that the power of evil is real in the present and can be expected in the future. But what is more important is that the authority of Jesus Christ is greater than the power of the evil one, both in the present and in the future. Jesus Christ is not only the victor over death and the liberator of those held in the bondage of sin, but he is also the victor over Satan.

Paul takes the existence of Satan seriously, as moral personal will against the will of God at the cosmic level of creation; but Satan's power is bounded, just as sin and death are bounded by the Lord Jesus Christ.

These difficult sentences have been the source of some controversy in the church, but the central teaching is clear. John Calvin's observation is to the point. "Paul confirms what he has said by an argument of contraries. For as anti-christ cannot stand otherwise than through the impostures of Satan, he must necessarily vanish as soon as Christ shines forth. In time, as it is only in darkness that he reigns, the dawn of the day puts to flight and extinguishes the thick darkness of his reign."

Additional Notes

See the discussion of the identity of, and biblical vocabulary concerning, the devil in E. F. Palmer's commentary *1, 2, 3 John and Revelation* [Waco, Tex.: Word, 1982], pp. 202 ff.

Raymond C. Kelcy offers a detailed discussion of the *man of lawlessness* reference, pp. 160–64. "This Lawless one may be a movement, an institution, a system, or even an individual. Whatever may be his exact identity, his doom is certain" (p. 164). See also the discussion by H. J. Ockenga (pp. 116–18).

The "lean is better than luxurious" rule for biblical interpretation is explained more fully in E. F. Palmer's commentary *1, 2, 3 John and Revelation*, pp. 121 ff.

15

A Firm Hope

2 THESSALONIANS 2:13–3:5

We must thank God at all times for you, brothers, you whom the Lord loves. For God chose you as the first[b] to be saved by the Spirit's power to make you his holy people and by your faith in the truth. [14]God called you to this through the Good News we preached to you; he called you to possess your share of the glory of our Lord Jesus Christ. [15]So then, our brothers, stand firm and hold on to those truths which we taught you, both in our preaching and in our letter.

[16]May our Lord Jesus Christ himself and God our Father, who loved us and in his grace gave us unfailing courage and a firm hope, [17]encourage you and strengthen you to always do and say what is good.

[1]Finally, our brothers, pray for us that the Lord's message may continue to spread rapidly and be received with honor, just as it was among you. [2]Pray also that God will rescue us from wicked and evil people; for not everyone believes the message. [3]But the Lord is faithful, and he will strengthen you and keep you safe from the Evil One. [4]And the Lord gives us confidence in you, and we are sure that you are doing and will continue to do what we tell you. [5]May the Lord lead you into a greater understanding of God's love and the endurance that is given by Christ.

b. as the first; *some manuscripts have* from the beginning.

2:13 / **For God chose you**: Paul continues to give thanks to God for these Christian friends at Thessalonica. They were chosen. The word translated **chose** is *haireomai*. This word is used in the New Testament only here in this text and in two others: Philippians 1:22, "If it is to be life in the flesh, that means fruitful labor for me. Yet which I shall *choose* I cannot tell"; and Hebrews 11:25, "*Choosing* rather to share ill-treatment with the people of God." In 2 Thess. 2:13 the word conveys a very deliberate, concrete, and definite sense of choice by God. Just as God's love for us is definite and concrete rather than vague and theoretical, so God's choice has that same concreteness.

Paul does not intend by this statement to imply that our freedom has been tampered with by God. Both of these letters have strongly affirmed the freedom of choice of the Thessalonian Christians at each stage of their Christian journey. Freedom has been a major thread from the beginning

of that journey—"You turned away from idols to God" (1 Thess. 1:9)—
and freedom continues as a major thread in the midst of their discipleship:
"So, then, our brothers, stand firm and hold on to these truths" (1 Thess.
2:15). God's authority never cancels out human freedom, whether for the
nonbeliever or for the believer. When a man or a woman trusts in Jesus
Christ as Lord, the result of the life of discipleship is not a lessening of
freedom or choices or responsibility; it is quite the reverse. The way of
discipleship intensifies the choices that we are to make; so much more is
now at stake that our choices matter all the more. It was Jesus who taught
this, in one of his most important parables: "Well done, good and faithful
servant; you have been faithful over a few things; I will make you ruler
over many; enter into the joy of your Lord" (Matt. 25:21). But if *our*
freedom is preserved by God, so also is *his* freedom. These two great facts
stand together and must never be compromised: the freedom of God and
the freedom of human beings; God's freedom, our freedom—they both
exist because of God's decision.

We must beware of any theological system that compromises either
God's freedom or human freedom. Beware of a theology that brings God
under its control; beware of a theology or a system of ethics that brings
men and women under its control. Only God himself has the right to reign
and to choose. One of his sovereign choices is to grant us the right to our
own choices; but the fact remains that there is no equation of God's freedom with our freedom. God's freedom is prior and sovereign; therefore,
our freedom depends upon it. God's decision stands before our choices
and, indeed, makes them possible.

As the first to be saved: There is a textual dilemma in this phrase,
and it has to do with the word translated **first**. Exactly what Greek word
or words has Paul used in this sentence? The GNB text offers the word
aparchē, literally "first fruits." But many ancient manuscripts offer two
words at this point, *ap'archēs*, which would then be translated "as first"
or "from the beginning." James Moffatt, in his translation, as well as the
New American Bible, prefer the term "first fruits;" however, the GNB
favors the term **as the first**. The King James, RSV, New International,
Jerusalem Bible, and ASV offer the translation "from the beginning."

The best manuscript evidence supports "first fruits" as the word
choice. Also, from the standpoint of literary criticism, there is the fact that
the term "first fruits" is a favorite Pauline term, as we know from his use
of it in his other books (Rom. 8:23; 11:16; 16:5; 1 Cor. 15:20, 23; 16:15).
What Paul is saying on this reading is that God chose the Thessalonians
as the first fruits to be saved in their city.

Paul has two great purposes in mind here. First, he wants these Christians to understand their own belovedness and worth. Listen to the language: "**God *chose* you to be *saved* to make you his *holy* people to possess your share of the *glory*.**"

2:15-16 / Paul's second purpose is to encourage these Christians to live out in the here and now these great prior facts, to share with the world what God has done in their lives: **So then, our brothers, stand firm and hold on to those truths.** Paul then prays for these friends: **May our Lord . . . who gave us courage and a firm hope, encourage you and strengthen you to always do and say what is good.** These Christians have been blessed and now must be a blessing to the world around them.

3:1 / **Finally . . . pray for us.** Paul now asks these friends to be a blessing to him and the Christians at Corinth. He asks for their prayers, to the end that the good news may continue to spread. There is a mystery in the speed of the gospel; Paul is well aware that it takes more than the sincerity or the preparation of the preachers, though he is one who insists upon both: there is a mystery involved in the witness of the believers, and that mystery is the confirmation of God himself.

The Holy Spirit must authenticate the message of salvation. Paul had earlier made this very affirmation. "God chose you as the first fruits to be saved *by the Spirit's power* to make you his holy people" (2:13). The Holy Spirit must confirm the witness of God's people so that it makes sense to a listener, and the Holy Spirit must make the message of the good news alive and redemptive in the life of a human being. Our task is to bear witness to the truth, but it is God's task to make the living and healing connection of that good news in the total life of an enquirer.

3:2-3 / Paul also asks for the prayers of his friends that he and his companions at Corinth might be protected from evil and assures them of his prayer for their protection from the **Evil One**, that is, Satan.

Paul is realistic about the dangers in the first-century Roman world, but he is not terrified. There is no panic in these letters. Paul is no "survivalist," trying to find a safe fortress; he is an adventurer, fully aware of the real dangers yet not prepared to allow those dangers to grind him to a halt. This is the stance of discipleship that Paul advocates for his Christian friends at Thessalonica too, and he assures them of his prayers on their behalf so that they will stay encouraged.

Paul believes in prayer. It is like the breathing of the Christian; it is fellowship between Christians and our Lord. Paul must have prayed for many people and situations, because every letter tells of his prayers for real people in real places. One of the reasons the apostle's mind is so clear and focused is that prayer has that benefit as a side effect. Prayer not only keeps our relationship warm and real, it keeps our total selves alert and clearheaded because of how deeply we care about what is going on around us. Best of all, our care is founded upon God's care. There is a solid basis in reality from which to pray and live.

Steadfastness is a major theme in Paul. The word choice of Paul in verse 3 is *pistos*, and it means "worthy of belief and trust." In other words, "The Lord is to be trusted." The same word was used in verse 2 with reference to the believers and our faith. It is therefore a play on words. We need faith, *pistos*, and God is faithful, *pistos*; he is the one upon whom we may put our faith. Paul makes that faithfulness teaching seem all the more emphatic by his use of the word *hypomenē*, "steadfast," "patient," at the close of verse 5. Christ is steadfast and solid. This word usually carries the sense of endurance as in 1 Thessalonians 1:3 and 2 Thessalonians 1:4. But here it is used in a more expansive sense; it shows the full and complete permanence of Jesus Christ as our faithful Lord. His faithfulness will endure. The Old Testament promise of Psalm 100 is fulfilled in Christ: "For the Lord is good; his steadfast love endures. . . . "

Additional Note

There are excellent discussions of the faith vocabulary of Paul in Best, pp. 329–31, and in Moore, pp. 112, 113. Since the Christians in Thessalonica are a persecuted community, "They are to take heart and strength for the assurance that God is faithful" (Moore, p. 112). It is clear in all biblical teaching about the character of God that his character remains trustworthy and dependable. This is the meaning of the Hebrew *amen* and becomes the foundation stone to all New Testament teaching on faith. Therefore, in the Bible "faith" is not an art form or a skillful achievement of boldness on the part of the believer, but it is the response of the believer to the evidence that is discovered of the faithfulness of God's character. Our human response, however tentative or shy, is the trust of our lives upon God's trustworthiness. It is that trust that is faith in the Bible. Therefore, the word is not a static term but dynamic in the fullest degree. Faith begins; it grows; it experiences ups and downs; it is never absolute; it puts its weight down on the faithfulness of God. Our faith is not absolute since God is the only absolute.

16

Marching Orders

2 THESSALONIANS 3:6–18

Our brothers, we command you in the name of our Lord Jesus Christ to keep away from all brothers who are living a lazy life and who do not follow the instructions that we gave them. [7]You yourselves know very well that you should do just what we did. We were not lazy when we were with you. [8]We did not accept anyone's support without paying for it. Instead, we worked and toiled; we kept working day and night so as not to be an expense to any of you. [9]We did this, not because we do not have the right to demand our support; we did it to be an example for you to follow. [10]While we were with you, we used to tell you, "Whoever refuses to work is not allowed to eat."

[11]We say this because we hear that there are some people among you who live lazy lives and who do nothing except meddle in other people's business. [12]In the name of the Lord Jesus Christ we command these people and warn them to lead orderly lives and work to earn their own living.

[13]But you, brothers, must not become tired of doing good. [14]It may be that someone there will not obey the message we send you in this letter. If so, take note of him and have nothing to do with him, so that he will be ashamed. [15]But do not treat him as an enemy; instead, warn him as a brother.

[16]May the Lord himself, who is our source of peace, give you peace at all times and in every way. The Lord be with you all.

[17]With my own hand I write this: *Greetings from Paul.* This is the way I sign every letter; this is how I write.

[18]May the grace of our Lord Jesus Christ be with you all.

3:6–10 / Paul once again makes use of the dramatic word *parangellō*, the same word used in his mandate exhortations of 1 Thessalonians 4:2 and 4:11. The escapism of some of the members of the fellowship has taken on such severe proportions that Paul is advocating strong measures in order to draw these people back to a useful and responsible stance. They have left their posts of daily work and daily discipleship, and Paul does not want the church to support them in this irresponsibility; hence the stern advice, **whoever refuses to work is not allowed to eat**.

On the positive side, the apostle boldly offers his own life as a model. He reminds them of his time at Thessalonica and of the way he and Silas lived in their city. He calls his life an example. The Greek is *mimeomai*, from which we have the English word *mimic*. It is a fact that a person needs to watch and be watched in order to learn. This is true for all kinds of learning. Small children learn by observing their parents' behavior. A skier needs to watch a downhill turn and then to be watched in turn as he or she tries to execute the turn. Paul is aware of this principle.

3:13-15 / This is the kind of salty counsel that is necessary when a family or a church becomes indulgent toward its own members, so that not only are self-destructive patterns excused, but the individuals involved are supported in those patterns. Paul calls for the cessation of this indulgence, and yet he warns against excessive severity: **Do not treat him as an enemy; instead, warn him as a brother**.

For Paul, it is a very important matter that Christians stay at their posts and actively pursue their life and faith within the normal cycle of real existence. No cloud-cuckoo-land spirituality for Paul! He wants Christians to be real people in real places, people who have jobs and family obligations, ethical responsibilities, and a clear sense of mission. His strong suspicion is that troublesome meddling is in direct proportion to a person's time away from his or her post of responsibility.

3:16 / Now Paul brings his letter to a close with the concern for **peace** in the life of the church, the **peace** that has its **source** in **the Lord himself**. This church needs the health and healing of God's peace because there has developed within the fellowship a hysterical faction. Paul's counsel is crisp and to the point, not labored or excessive. Now he encircles his pastoral counsel with his prayer for God's peace for God's people at Thessalonica.

3:17 / **With my own hand**: The apostle takes the pen from his secretary who up until now has been writing the letter from Paul's dictation. Paul writes his own final greeting to the document, as is his normal custom, and then informs his readers that this is his personal signature. His explicit note may be due to the problem at Thessalonica of the spurious letter that had been claimed by false prophets as coming from Paul.

3:18 / Having wished peace to his readers, Paul now joins that prayer on their behalf with his prayer for **the grace of our Lord Jesus Christ**. So Paul ends his letters as he began them; grace and peace surround Paul's first letters to the Christians because grace and peace surround the Christians.

Additional Note

3:17 / We have evidence from another letter that Paul made use of secretaries to assist him in the writing of his letters. One of those writers identifies himself directly in Rom. 16:22: "I Tertius, the writer of this letter greet you in the Lord." Also, in Paul's greeting in the Letter to the Galatians he draws attention to this procedure with his aside, "See with what large letters I am writing to you with my own hand" (Gal. 6:11).

Epilogue: Why Be a Christian?

Paul did not try to convert anyone to Christianity in the two letters to the Thessalonians that he wrote in A.D. 51, yet there is a persuasive quality to these letters. If you are a non-Christian who is watching this young church in action, you will make some very significant discoveries that will help you in making up your mind about the credibility of the Christian faith.

First of all, Paul's letters to the Thessalonians have established the fact that whatever else Christianity is, it has to do with *real people in a real place*. They live their lives in the times and culture of all other human beings in the human story. Christian faith is historical and concrete. The believer, in believing in Christ, is not disconnected from historical life, with its daily cycle of work and play, of suffering and joy, of life beginning and life ending.

When the people at Thessalonica believe in the gospel, it means that for them the meaning of their lives is derived from the decision that God made about life rather than from the influence of the dominant Roman or Greek culture. But that decision from God does not lead them away from culture into the spooky mists of spiritualism. The first sentence of the book is clear on this question; it is addressed to the people *at Thessalonica* (1 Thess. 1:1). The Christians are never urged in this book to leave Thessalonica or to abandon its crises. Whatever faith means in these books, it is clear that it is meant to work right where the people live. It seems to me that this is important to know if a person is looking into the claims of Jesus Christ. It means that the effect of those claims and promises is to be experienced by a person here and now. Christian faith as taught in 1 and 2 Thessalonians is plainly and inescapably historical.

The second great discovery that a reader makes in these two letters is that there is no mistaking what for Paul is the center of his faith. Paul is a man in Christ; it is Jesus Christ who has won Paul's respect and faith. We learn from Paul in these letters that the Christ of his faith is the Jesus of history: "For since we believe that Jesus died and rose again . . ." (1 Thess. 4:14). Paul's faith and hope are not directed toward a phantom redeemer or an inhabitant of the spirit world but toward the concrete Jesus of Nazareth, who identified totally with humanity in the companionship of the road and even in the loneliness of death.

Paul is confident that this same Jesus has conquered death with the same realism and actuality as he endured death. The death and the resurrection of Jesus Christ is for Paul "total help for total need" (Barth). Just as we are real and live our lives in a real world, so the Lord Jesus Christ is real. All escapism from this reality of history is foreign to Paul both in his theology and in his ethics. Paul also affirms throughout these letters that this Jesus Christ of history is alive and reigns and will come again as the boundary of history at its end, as he does at its beginning and has radically entered at its center.

The best part of Paul's letters are his sentences about the love and faithfulness of Jesus Christ. Paul believes that Christ's love and faithfulness are real and practical and therefore knowable by men and women.

The third discovery that we make in Paul's letters to the Thessalonians has to do with the implications of faith in Jesus Christ. If we are to believe in this Lord, there will be a change in our life. Paul teaches that the Holy Spirit, who confirms the reality of Christ to us, also changes our motivation and our self-understanding. The Holy Spirit does not cancel out our freedom—in fact, our freedom is intensified—but the Holy Spirit fills us with the living companionship of Christ (1 Thess. 1:2–10).

In Paul's way of looking at this, the results are far-reaching and demanding. Christ as our Shepherd-Lord calls us to the way of righteousness. This call has direct implications in our marriages, our work, our personal relationships (1 Thess. 4:12).

Another discovery we make in these letters is that the Christian church itself is in continual need of renewal and correction. As a reader of these letters, I have discovered that the church as a fellowship is not within itself absolute; in fact, it often goes astray, so that it must be repeatedly called back to its good center, Jesus Christ himself.

Even this discovery is in the end an encouragement, because it protects the potential Christian believer from any tendency toward the deification of the church. I should not expect too much from the fellowship of believers; they cannot be an absolute guidance system for me, because I recognize in Paul's letters how possible it is that they, like me, may go astray. But knowing this, I then see the fellowship of believers for the wonderful resource that it really is. In that ancient and contemporary fellowship I find companions on the way who need the Savior as much as I do, who need to grow as much as I, and yet who are sharing in the grace and the companionship of the same Lord.

Though Paul has not set out in his letters to win over the skeptic and the non-Christian reader, his book has done it because he was good enough to point on every page to Jesus Christ the Lord of the center and the friend of the way.

Abbreviations

ASV	American Standard Version
BAG	William F. Arndt and F. Wilbur Gingrich. *A Greek-English Lexicon*. Translated by Walter Bauer
DSB	Daily Study Bible
GNB	Good News Bible
HNTC	Harper's New Testament Commentary
ICC	The International Critical Commentary
ISBE	*The International Standard Bible Encyclopaedia*
LS	H. G. Liddell and R. Scott. *Greek-English Lexicon*. 1940
LWC	Living Word Commentary
MM	J. H. Moulton and G. Milligan. *The Vocabulary of the Greek New Testament*
MNTC	Moffatt New Testament Commentary
NBD	*The New Bible Dictionary*. 1962
NCB	The New Century Bible Commentary
NICNT	The New International Commentary on the New Testament
NIDNTT	Colin Brown, ed. *The New International Dictionary of New Testament Theology*
RSV	Revised Standard Version
TDNT	Gerhard Kittel and George Friedrich, eds. *Theological Dictionary of the New Testament*
WBC	World Biblical Commentary

For Further Reading

Commentaries on 1 and 2 Thessalonians

Barclay, William. *The Letters to the Philippians, Colossians, and Thessalonians*. Daily Study Bible. Philadelphia: Westminster Press, 1975.

Best, Ernest. *The First and Second Epistles to the Thessalonians*. Harper's New Testament Commentaries. New York: Harper & Row, 1972.

Bruce, F. F. *1 & 2 Thessalonians*. World Bible Commentary. Waco, Tex.: Word, 1982.

Calvin, John. *The Epistles of Paul the Apostle to the Romans and Thessalonians*. Calvin's New Testamant Commentaries (Torrance edition). Grand Rapids, Mich.: Eerdmans, 1948.

Frame, James E. *A Critical and Exegetical Commentary on the Epistles of St. Paul to the Thessalonians*. The International Critical Commentary on the Holy Scriptures of the Old and New Testaments. New York: C. Scribner's Sons, 1912.

Hubbard, David Alan. *Thessalonians: Life That's Radically Christian*. Waco, Tex.: Word Books, 1977.

Kelcy, Raymond C. *Letters of Paul to the Thessalonians*. Living Word Commentary. Austin, Tex.: R. B. Sweet, 1977.

Milligan, George. *St. Paul's Epistle to the Thessalonians: The Greek Text*. New York: Macmillan Co., 1908.

Moore, A. L. *1 and 2 Thessalonians*. New Century Bible. London: Marshall, Morgan, & Scott, 1969.

Morris, Leon. *Epistles of Paul to the Thessalonians*. Tyndale New Testament Commentaries. Grand Rapids, Mich.: Eerdmans, 1956.

Morris, Leon, ed. and trans. *First and Second Epistles to the Thessalonians*. New International Commentary on the New Testament/New London Commentary on the New Testament. London: Marshall, Morgan and Scott, 1959.

Neil, William. *Epistle of Paul to the Thessalonians*. Moffatt New Testament Commentary. New York: Harper & Row, 1950.

Ockenga, Harold J. *The Epistles to the Thessalonians*. Grand Rapids, Mich.: Baker, 1962.

Ward, Ronald A. *Commentary on 1 & 2 Thessalonians*. Waco, Tex.: Word Books, 1973.

Whiteley, D. E. H. "Introduction" and "Commentary" in *Thessalonians in the Revised Standard Version*. New Clarendon Bible, New Testament. London: Oxford University Press, 1969.

Books on Paul

Barclay, William. *The Mind of St. Paul*. Toronto: William Collins Sons & Co., 1958.

Bruce, F. F. *The Letters of Paul*. Grand Rapids, Mich.: Eerdmans, 1965.

Bruce, F. F. *Paul: Apostle of the Heart Set Free*. Grand Rapids, Mich.: Eerdmans, 1977.

Bultmann, Rudolf. "The Theology of Paul," in *Theology of the New Testament*. Translated by Kendrick Grobel. New York: Scribner, 1952.

Deissmann, Adolf. *Paul: A Study in Social and Religious History*. 2nd ed. Translated by William E. Wilson. London: Hodder and Stoughton, 1926.

Dodd. C. H. *Epistle of Paul to the Romans*. Moffatt New Testament Commentary. New York: Harper & Brothers, 1932.

Drane, John W. *Paul*. Berkhamsted, England: Lion Pub., 1977.

Furnish, Victor Paul. *Theology and Ethics in Paul*. Nashville, Tenn.: Abingdon Press, 1968.

Glover, T. R. *Paul of Tarsus*. London: Student Christian Movement, 1925.

Hunter, A. M. *Interpreting Paul's Gospel*. (Union Theological Seminary. James Sprunt Lectures, 1954.) London: Student Christian Movement Press, 1954.

Longenecker, Richard N. *Paul, Apostle of Liberty*. New York: Harper & Row, 1964.

Nock, Arthur Darby. *St. Paul*. London: T. Butterworth, 1938.

Ramsay, William M. *St. Paul the Traveller and the Roman Citizen* (with essay by W. Ward Gasque). Twin Brook Series (reprint of 1925 ed.). Grand Rapids, Mich.: Baker Book House, 1982.

Ridderbos, Herman N. *Paul: An Outline of His Theology*. Translated by John Richard de Witt. Grand Rapids, Mich.: Eerdmans, 1975.

Rigaux, Béda. *The Letters of St. Paul*. Edited and translated by Stephen Yonick. Chicago: Franciscan Herald Press, 1968.

Sandmel, Samuel. *The Genius of Paul: A Study in History*. New York: Schocken Books, 1970.

Scroggs, Robin. *Paul for a New Day*. Philadelphia: Fortress Press, 1966.

Stacey, W. D. *The Pauline View of Man: In Relation to Its Judaic and Hellenistic Background*. New York: St. Martins Press, 1956.

Stendahl, Krister. *Paul Among Jews and Gentiles, and Other Essays*. Philadelphia: Fortress Press, 1976.

Stewart, James S. *A Man in Christ: Vital Elements in St. Paul's Religion.* New York: Harper, 1935.

Whiteley, D. E. H. *The Theology of St. Paul.* Philadelphia: Fortress Press, 1964.

Other Works

Barclay, William, ed. and trans. *The Letters of John.* Daily Study Bible. Philadelphia: Westminster Press, 1958.

Barr, James. *Biblical Words for Time.* (Studies in Biblical Theology, No. 33.) Naperville, Ill.: Alec E. Allenson, 1962.

Barth, Karl. *Dogmatics in Outline.* Translated by G. T. Thompson. New York: Harper, 1949.

Bonhoeffer, Dietrich. *The Cost of Discipleship.* Translated by R. H. Fuller. New York: MacMillan, 1948.

Bonhoeffer, Dietrich. *Letters and Papers from Prison.* Edited by Eberhard Bethge. Translated by R. H. Fuller. London: Student Christian Movement Press, 1953.

Brown, Colin, ed. *The New International Dictionary of New Testament Theology.* 3 vols. Grand Rapids, Mich.: Zondervan Pub. House, 1975–78.

Bruce, F. F. *Answers to Questions.* Grand Rapids, Mich.: Zondervan Pub. House, 1973.

Bruce, F. F. *New Testament History.* Garden City, N.Y.: Doubleday, 1971.

Bultmann, Rudolf. *Primitive Christianity in its Contemporary Setting.* Translated by R. H. Fuller. New York: Meridian Books, 1956.

Chesterton, G. K. *The Everlasting Man.* London: Hodder and Stoughton, 1936.

Cullmann, Oscar. *Christ and Time.* London: Student Christian Movement Press, 1951.

Grant, Robert M. *Augustus to Constantine: The Thrust of the Christian Movement into the Roman World.* New York: Harper & Row, 1970.

Kittel, Gerhard, and Georg Friedrich, eds. *Theological Dictionary of the New Testament.* 10 vols. Grand Rapids, Mich.: Eerdmans, 1954–76.

Lewis, C. S. *Miracles.* New York: MacMillan, 1947.

Lewis, C. S. *The Weight of Glory.* New York: MacMillan, 1949.

Morris, Leon. *The Cross in the New Testament.* Grand Rapids, Mich.: Eerdmans, 1965.

Moulton, James Hope, and George Milligan. *The Vocabulary of the Greek New Testament*. London and New York: Hodder and Stoughton, 1930.

Piper, Otto. *Christian Ethics*. Camden, N.Y.: Thomas Nelson and Sons, 1970.

Richardson, Cyril, ed. and trans. *Early Christian Fathers*. New York: MacMillan, 1970.

Rowley, H. H. *From Moses to Qumran: Studies in the Old Testament*. New York: Association Press, 1963.

Subject Index

Adelphos, meaning of term, 10, 13
"After Ten Years," 45
Agapē, meaning of word, 6–7
Aiōn, use of word, 41
Akribōs, use of word, 42–43
Alexander the Great, xvi
Amen, meaning of, 72
Apokalypsis, use of word, 62
Apolinarius, 1
Apollos, 36
Apollyōn, 66
Apostasia, use of word, 65
Apostle: concept of, 16; Paul as, 16; use of term, 16
Ataktos, use of word, 52
Athens, xvi
Augustine, Saint, 25, 26

Barclay, William, xix, 1
Barr, James, 41
Barth, Karl, 9, 61, 76
Baur, F. C., 3
Believers already dead, fate of, 34, 35; Paul's answer to, 39
Best, Ernest, 4, 60, 63, 72
Bonhoeffer, Dietrich, 7, 9, 22, 27, 45
Brothers, meaning of term, 10, 13
Brown, Raymond, xx
Bruce, F. F., xix, 66
Bultmann, Rudolf, 38
"Burnout," 53

Calvin, John, 25, 66, 67
Chara, use of word, 54
Charge, use of word, 24
Charis, 2, 4
Chesterton, G. K., 49
Chosen, Thessalonians as, 69
Christ. *See* Jesus Christ
The Christian Interpretation of Sex, 28
Chronos vs. *kairos*, use, 41–42
Chrysostom, 66
Church: beginnings of, in Thessalonica, xvi–xviii, 12–16; as God's joy, 63; as scandal, 63
Claudius, xv
Clouse, Robert, 45–46
Comforted, meaning of word, 15
Commentary on the Letters of John and Jude, 1
Conrad, Joseph, 9
Costly grace, love as, 7
Crown of pride, boasting, meaning of phrase, 20

Day of the Lord: timing of, 47, 48, 65; use of phrase, 43
Dead, believers already, fate of, 34, 35; Paul's answer to, 39
Dead Sea Scrolls, xvii
Destruction, meaning of word, 47

Diabolos, 66
Dikaios, use of word, 61
Dodd, C. H., 11, 36
Dokimazō, use of word, 54–55
Doxa, meaning of word, 14, 19
Durant, Will, 27

Eidōlon, meaning of word, 9
Eirēnē, meaning of word, 2
Ekdikos, use of word, 26
Ekklēsia, meaning of term, 1
Eliot, T. S., 9
Elpis, use of word, 7
Encourage one another, Christians to, 49
Energeia, use of word, 18
Epithumia, meaning of word, 26
Ergon, use of word, 6, 18
Escapism, Christians to avoid, 47–50, 55–56, 73–74, 76–77
Essenes, xvii
Ethic of Paul, 59
The Ethics of Sex, 28
Euangelion, use of word, 13
Eucharistoumen, use of word, 5
Euodia, 15
Extended family of believers, love for, 30–32

Faith: of Thessalonians, 58–59; as work, 6, 18, 59
Faith vocabulary of Paul, 72
Family language, use, 19
Father, as term for God, 1–2, 4
First fruits vs. first, choice of word, 70
Freedom: of believer, allowed by God, 8–9, 66–67, 69–70, 77; of God, 70

Galatians, letter to, date of, xix
Gallio, xix
Gnosticism, 35–38; warnings against, 36, 38
Good News, 9; as of God, 17–18; meaning of term, 13
Grace: meaning of word, 2; use of word, 4
Grace and peace, 74; as mark of Paul, 2, 58
Greek ideas, in Christianity, 36
Greeting, formal style of, 1, 58
Guthrie, D., xix

Hagiasmos, use of word, 25
Haireomai, use of word, 69
The Heart of Darkness, 9
Hell, as defined by Paul, 62
High Priestly Prayer of Jesus, 40
Hippolytus, 36
Holiness, 28–29; and love, as whole of Christian activity, 23; meaning of word, 25. *See also* Holy
Holistic understanding of personality, 55–56
"The Hollow Men," 9
Holoteleis, use of word, 56

Holy, honorable, marriage as, 27–28
Holy Spirit, 7, 8, 15, 23, 29, 40, 54–55, 65, 71, 77
Homeiromai, use of word, 14
Hope: in Jesus, 7; Thessalonians as Paul's, 19
Ho poneros, 66
The Horse and His Boy, 54
Hort, 15
Hyper-ex-perissou, use of word, 52
Hypomonē, use of word, 7, 72

Idle, warning to, 52
Idols, turning away from, 8–10, 10–11
Imitate, meaning of word, 10
Irenaeus, 1, 36, 37, 38
Isaiah, xix

Jason, xviii, 14
Jeremiah, xix
Jesus Christ: as already returned, 35, 37, 38; as center of faith, 39, 43–45, 49, 55, 76; as judge, 62; timing of return, 34, 35, 37, 38, 41–50
Jews, as persecutors, 18–19; meaning of term, 20
Joel, 16
John, xix, 10
John the Baptist, xvii, xx
Joy: importance of, 54; Thessalonians as Paul's, 19
Judgment of God, 61–63
Justin Martyr, 36
Juvenal, 27

Kairos vs. *chronos,* use, 41–42
Kalos, use of word, 55
Katechō, use of word, 65
Kelcy, Raymond C., 67
Kingdom language, 60
Kiss, believers to greet with, 56
Kittel, Gerhard, 26
Koimaō, meaning of word, 38
Kolakia, use of word, 14
Kopos, use of word, 6
Kyrios, meaning of word, 2

Lazarus, 38
Leaders, Thessalonians to respect, 51–52
"Lean is better than luxurious" rule, 67, 68
Letters and Papers from Prison, 22
Letters to Thessalonians: date of, xvi, xix; purpose of, xv
Lewis, C. S., 9, 54, 60
Light, people of the, 47, 48
Lord, meaning of word, 2
Love: as costly grace, 7; and holiness, as whole of Christian activity, 23; marching order on, 31–32, 52; as present among Thessalonians, 58–59; as work, 6–7, 59
"The Love Song of J. Alfred Prufrock," 9
Luke, xvi, xvii, xviii, 15, 16

Makrothumeō, use of word, 53, 56
Malachi, xvii

Man of lawlessness, 65, 67–68
Marching orders, 24, 30, 31–32, 73–74
Marcus the Valentinian, 37
Marriage: Christian, 24–29; marching order on, 31; in Roman society, 27
Martin, R. P., xix
Maurer, Professor, 26
Messiah, Jewish expectation of, xvii, xix–xx
Military language, use, 24, 49, 52
Milligan, George, 15, 25, 51, 52
Mimeomai, use of word, 73
Miracles, 10
Moffatt, James, 26, 40, 70
Moore, A. L., 72
Morris, Leon, 60, 66, 67
Moses, 4
Moulton, James Hope, 51

Nag Hammadi manuscripts, 36, 37
Name, significance of, 63
Neil, William, 11, 32, 60
Nero, xv, 27
Nursery language, use, 14–15

Ockenga, H. J., 68
Oida, use of word, 51
1, 2, 3 John and Revelation, 67, 68

Palmer, E. F., 67, 68
Parakeleō, meaning of word, 15, 40
Parangellō, use of word, 24, 73
Parousia, use of word, 62
Patience, importance of, 53, 56
Paul: as Apostle, 16; as author of these lettes, xv, xvi, 3–4; characteristics as writer, xix; chronology of life, 3; ethics of, 59; faith vocabulary of, 72; as Greek, Jew, and Roman, xix, 4; as missional, 16, 32; and prayer, 5–6, 71–72; strategy of ministry, 22–23; in Thessalonica, xvi–xvii, xviii, 13, 14; use of secretaries, 75; as writer of final greeting, 74, 75
Peace: meaning of term, 2; need for at Thessalonica, 52, 74. *See also* Grace and peace
Persecutions suffered, 18, 59–60
Peter, 16, 36
Pharisees, 4
Philadelphia, meaning of word, 30–31
Philotimeomai, use of word, 32
Piper, Otto, 28, 59
Pistos, use of word, 72
Politarchēs, use of term, xviii
Porneia, meaning of word, 25
Prayer, and Paul, 5–6, 71–72
Priscilla, 36
Proseuchomai, use of word, 5

Rebellion, use of word, 65
Respect for leaders, need for, 51–52
Restrainer of lawless one, meaning of phrase, 65–66

Satan, 66–67, 71

Scripture Index